The Economics of Freedom

What is freedom? Can we measure it? Does it affect policy? This book develops an original measure of freedom called *autonomy freedom*, consistent with J. S. Mill's view of autonomy, and applies it to issues in policy and political design. The work pursues three aims. First, it extends classical liberalism beyond exclusive reliance on negative freedom so as to take autonomous behavior explicitly into account. Second, it develops firm conceptual foundations for a new standard in the measurement of freedom that can be fruitfully coupled with existing gauges. Third, it shows empirically that individual preferences for redistribution and cross-country differences in welfare spending in Organisation for Economic Cooperation and Development (OECD) countries are driven by the degree of autonomy freedom that individuals enjoy. By means of an interdisciplinary approach and a sophisticated econometric methodology, the book takes an explicit stand in defense of freedom and sets the basis for a liberalism based upon people, actions, and institutions.

Sebastiano Bavetta is professor of economics at the University of Palermo, Italy, and visiting professor of Economics and Philosophy at the University of Pennsylvania, USA. He is a research associate at the Centre for Philosophy of Natural and Social Science (CPNSS) at the London School of Economics (UK), where he obtained his Ph.D. in Philosophy of Economics. He has published in various international journals and has coauthored a book in Italian (*Liberalism in the Age of Conflict*, 2008). His research interests focus on policy and institutional design and on the measurement of freedom and its policy and political implications. He has extensive political and administrative experience in Italian local governmental agencies.

Pietro Navarra is professor of public economics at the University of Messina, Italy, where he is also Deputy Vice-Chancellor in charge of the budget. He is also visiting professor at the University of Pennsylvania, USA, and a research associate at the Centre for Philosophy of Natural and Social Science (CPNSS) at the London School of Economics (UK). He holds a Ph.D. in economics from the University of Buckingham, UK. Professor Navarra coedited with Ram Mudambi and Giuseppe Sobbrio *Rules and Reason: Perspectives on Constitutional Political Economy* (Cambridge University Press, 2001) and coauthored with them *Rules, Choice, and Strategy: The Political Economy of Italian Electoral Reform* (2001). He has published more than 50 articles in journals such as the *Journal of International Business Studies, Public Choice, European Journal of Political Economy, Oxford Bulletin of Economics and Statistics, Economics of Governance*, and *Applied Economics*. His research interests embrace the measurement of freedom, the relation between political institutions and economic reform, and the interplay between individual empowerment, entrepreneurship and economic growth.

The Economics of Freedom

Theory, Measurement, and Policy Implications

SEBASTIANO BAVETTA

Università di Palermo, Italy, and London School of Economics and Political Science, UK

PIETRO NAVARRA

Università di Messina, Italy, and London School of Economics and Political Science, UK

CAMBRIDGE
UNIVERSITY PRESS

CAMBRIDGE
UNIVERSITY PRESS

Shaftesbury Road, Cambridge CB2 8EA, United Kingdom

One Liberty Plaza, 20th Floor, New York, NY 10006, USA

477 Williamstown Road, Port Melbourne, VIC 3207, Australia

314–321, 3rd Floor, Plot 3, Splendor Forum, Jasola District Centre, New Delhi – 110025, India

103 Penang Road, #05–06/07, Visioncrest Commercial, Singapore 238467

Cambridge University Press is part of Cambridge University Press & Assessment, a department of the University of Cambridge.

We share the University's mission to contribute to society through the pursuit of education, learning and research at the highest international levels of excellence.

www.cambridge.org
Information on this title: www.cambridge.org/9781107017849

First published 2012

A catalogue record for this publication is available from the British Library

Library of Congress Cataloging-in-Publication data
Bavetta, Sebastiano, 1964–
The economics of freedom : theory, measurement, and policy implications / Sebastiano Bavetta, Pietro Navarra.
p. cm.
Includes bibliographical references and index.
ISBN 978-1-107-01784-9 (hardback)
1. Economics–Political aspects. 2. Liberty–Economic aspects.
3. Autonomy–Economic aspects. I. Navarra, Pietro. II. Title.
HB74.P65B38 2012
330–dc2   2012007321

ISBN   978-1-107-01784-9   Hardback

To our parents

Contents

List of tables and figures

TABLES

FIGURES

Preface

This book was conceived in London and traveled across four different continents before completion. It is therefore quintessentially about freedom since, beside being its subject matter, freedom figures prominently among its productive factors. Which freedom? Undoubtedly, the negative freedoms offered by the political and civil institutions developed by the Western civilization: freedom of movements, freedom of research, freedom of association in the pursuit of a common end – a scientific endeavor, in this case. None of the traveling and discussions that led to the ideas unfolded in these pages would have been possible without these freedoms.

Yet, freedom is as much about economic, political, and civil institutions as it is about finding a unique way to design, interpret, and implement one's own course in life. In *Capitalism and Freedom*, Milton Friedman said that "no frontiers of human knowledge and understanding, in literature, in technical possibilities, or in the relief of human misery, [have been achieved] in response to governmental directives. Their achievements were the product of individual genius, of strongly held minority views, of a social climate permitting variety and diversity." If institutions matter to the shape of freedom, more so does self-mastery, the affirmation of each person's unique identity and view of the good, the perception that we have to steer our way among the innumerable accidents and circumstances that characterize our days in this world. This latter kind of freedom, rooted in the idea of autonomy brilliantly crafted by the gifted pen of John Stuart Mill, constitutes an input of this book in a more pregnant sense than institutional freedom.

The reason is twofold. First, it is with a fully fulfilled sense of self-mastery that we shaped the particular discussion of freedom that the reader will find in these pages. Such a discussion is the outcome of an intellectual endeavor undertaken by two economists with solid interdisciplinary interests. Both of us developed our view of freedom in an unorthodox academic environment, the Centre for Philosophy of the Natural and Social Science at the London School of Economics, where philosophers, economists, and political scientists have the almost unique opportunity to reflect together, as if unconstrained by the artificial boundaries that limit the domain of their respective disciplines, upon questions that concern our social life. In this intellectual environment, fecund and open to cross-fertilization, we could develop – and personify, in this book – a unique view to approach the measurement of freedom and a singular, multidisciplinary approach to discuss freedom. We leave to the readers to decide whether our view is convincing beside being "eccentric."

Self-mastery is an input in another sense, too. For the last few years scholars have been engaged in the search for new foundations for national accounts. The physical measure offered by the GDP has plenty of merits, but it is unsatisfactory in a world informed by the competition of values where what we want to assess is well-being and where well-being is intrinsically pluralist. We believe that freedom must play a central role in this debate and, eventually, in the calculation of how people feel about their life. Yet, it can hardly enjoy such a centrality if its measurement goes no further than an assessment of institutional quality and overlooks each person's feeling to be in control of her own fate. So, whereas a measure of autonomy freedom is the output of this work, it is altogether an input for it informs the motivations of the authors and touches upon some relevant and unresolved questions in the social sciences.

Our central concern in this book is to answer three fundamental questions: What is freedom? Can we measure it? Does freedom affect policy choices? To respond to these questions, we develop an original measure of freedom consistent with the Millian view of autonomy and apply it to issues in policy and political design. In a nutshell, the book pursues three aims. First, it extends classical liberalism beyond exclusive reliance on the "voluntariness" aspect of negative freedom so as to take autonomous behavior explicitly into account. Second, it grounds on firm conceptual foundations a new standard in freedom measurement that can be fruitfully coupled with the existing rods of economic freedom. Third, it shows empirically that individual preferences for redistribution and cross-country differences in welfare spending in Organization for Economic Coordination and Development (OECD) countries are driven by the degree of autonomy freedom people enjoy. By means of an interdisciplinary approach, we take an explicit stand in defense of freedom and set the basis for a new perspective of liberalism based upon the centrality of the person *and* institutions.

The book was written with an interdisciplinary audience in mind: We hope that economists, political scientists, and philosophers are interested in its contents and in the debate we contribute to. Although the book can be used as supplementary reading in specially designed courses, it is particularly suited for programs in philosophy, politics, and economics at the graduate and upper undergraduate level.

The writing of this book spanned a long time, adding substantially to our intellectual obligations. We express our gratitude to the various academic institutions that hosted us during the various stages of the manuscript: the Centre for Philosophy of Natural and Social Science at the London School of Economics has already been mentioned. A fundamental contribution has been given by the two wonderful months we spent in the summer of 2008 at the Research School of Social Sciences at the Australian National University (ANU), in Canberra. Keith Dowding, a great host and a fierce debater, deserves our deepest appreciation for his patience and insights like all the people we talked to, in person or in seminars, at ANU. The Department of Economics at Fudan University, Shanghai, which we visited at the end of 2004, gave us the opportunity to present our measure of freedom to Chinese students. We are still fascinated by their enthusiastic response, unmatched anywhere else we brought discourses on freedom and its measurement. A particular mention is merited by the Philosophy, Politics, and Economics (PPE) program at the University of Pennsylvania. Colleagues, staff, and students in Locust Walk make up a congenial and intellectually stimulating environment where ideas and opinions are passionately and rigorously discussed. We taught the content of this book in the PPE's Capstone seminars and enjoyed the benefit of highly attentive, motivated, and intelligent students that contributed to make these pages better. We are also grateful to the students who attended our classes at the London School of Economics, at the University of Konstanz, at the University of Messina, and at the University of Bayreuth, who helped us to clarify our claims and to change convoluted arguments into straightforward ones.

Our deepest gratitude goes to our own institutions: the Universities of Palermo and Messina. Both of them provided encouragement and financial support for our research activity in a period in which neither encouragement nor support can be taken for granted.

The ideas contained in this book have been presented at many conferences, workshops, and seminars. While we bear full responsibility for any shortcoming, we have also benefited from discussions with friends and colleagues. Their number has grown too large for a complete listing, but we would like to name Pierluigi Barrotta, Luc Bovens, Ian Carter, Wulf Gaertner, Robert Goodin, Bernie Grofman, Russell Hardin, Martin van Hees, Chandran Kukathas, Ned McClennen, Terry Miller, William Niskanen, Emilio Pacheco, Prasanta Pattanaik, Vito Peragine, and Giuseppe Sobbrio for their thought-provoking criticisms in the various stages of the manuscript. With a deep sense of gratitude we thank Cristina Bicchieri and Nancy Cartwright for providing us with inspiring guidance and continuous encouragement to pursue our research agenda. We are especially indebted to Geoffrey Brennan, Francesco Guala, Ram Mudambi, Maurice Salles, and three anonymous referees for their insightful suggestions and extensive discussion of the book's content, which helped to strengthen our arguments and refine our ideas. We would also like to express our appreciation to Margherita Bottero and Dario Maimone Ansaldo Patti for their research assistance and their collaboration on two chapters of this book.

Sincere thanks are also due to Scott Parris, economics editor at Cambridge University Press, who supported us throughout the book's preparation. His constant confidence in our project was crucial to the book's completion. We thank also Adam Levine and the production team at Cambridge University Press. We owe them a great deal for shepherding us through the publication process.

Finally, no project of this magnitude can be accomplished without a substantial personal cost. Our families had to endure long and frequent absences while this project was under way, and we express our heartfelt thanks to them for bearing with us.

1

Introduction

The centrality of the idea of freedom in cultures and societies is undisputed; the meaning of freedom is essentially contested. Some scholars use this term to indicate a space where each individual may act as he likes; others refer to the exercise of autonomous judgment; others underline the development of an inner self; others equate freedom to availability of choices; and the list is not exhaustive.

Take the case of the United States. Although the idea of freedom is at the heart of the nation's creed, two different visions of individual liberty emerged in the twentieth century. The difference between them becomes most apparent when we compare their prescriptions in the touchy domain of social security. On the progressive camp, inspired by Franklin Delano Roosevelt's New Deal, the promotion of *freedom from want and fear* is not necessarily diminished by the intervention of the state; instead, it can often be advanced only through the vigorous action of government. In this perspective, economic fairness and distributive justice have been the guiding principles at the basis of the progressive conception of social security. Differently, on the conservative camp, individual liberty is affirmed in a civil society where the role of government is limited and families, neighborhoods, and faith communities sustain the moral foundations of freedom. In this view, public policies are based on three major ingredients: freedom of choice, individual responsibility, and freedom from government dependence. In the words of George W. Bush's second inaugural address, "in America's ideal of freedom the public interest depends on private character [...] Self-government relies, in the end, on the governing of the self."[1]

These two approaches to freedom and, eventually, social security have also largely characterized the competing political stands in Western industrialized economies. In this book we are not interested in the philosophical debate on the correct interpretation that should be attached to the word "freedom". We work in the classical liberal tradition and take the idea of negative freedom as a reference point. Following Berlin (1969), *negative freedom* is the absence of constraints, the conscious and unimpeded exercise in one's own private sphere of an agent's voluntariness. Negative freedom is contrasted with *positive freedom*, namely the possibility of acting so as to take control of one's life and realize one's fundamental purposes. We are interested in the kind of social security that our reading of negative freedom brings about. Our focus is therefore on a specific interpretation of the idea of negative freedom, on its foundations and measurement, and on its policy implications, with exclusive reference to social security and, more precisely, to the optimal size of the welfare state.

In the light of the two competing views of freedom in the domain of social security pinpointed earlier, our approach has many favorable features. First, social security is often at odds with negative freedom. Our approach allows us to reconcile the aspects of distributive justice and individual responsibility along the perspective of classical liberalism. This result should not be underestimated. We argue that individuals form their attitudes toward inequality on the basis of considerations about fairness concerned with the sources of wealth and poverty. These considerations focus on procedures and depend on the extent of freedom individuals enjoy. A wider freedom of choice and a firmer control over life outcomes associated with free choices strengthen individual responsibility and reduce the scope of state intervention to redress inequality. Nonegalitarian societies can then be as just as egalitarian societies if the process that leads to a given distribution of income is consistent with the degree of control that people perceive over the course that their lives take.

---

[1] A thoroughly discussion of the forms in which the idea of freedom materialized over time in the American society is offered by Foner (1998).

Second, many analyses of social security or the optimal size of the welfare state are conducted within the successful but limiting frame offered by political economy. This is unsatisfactory since people's protection through state intervention involves issues that often go beyond the structure of incentives that actors have under different characteristics and dimensions of the welfare state. An interdisciplinary approach is necessary to capture the individual motives that lead to different structures of social protection across societies and to draw precise prescriptive conclusions. Third, one has to acknowledge that, as the search for people's motives involves subjective testimony, a systematic approach is necessary to anchor the data offered by such a testimony to firm analytical foundations.

To open our journey on our interpretation of freedom and its measurement, we start with a sketch of the relationship between choice and the measurement of freedom.

1.1 CHOICE AND THE MEASUREMENT OF FREEDOM

According to Carter (1999), political philosophers have always been engaged in "an unashamedly trans-historical discussion" concerning the measurement of freedom (Hobbes, 1990; Hayek, 1960; Rawls, 1971). Even Berlin (1969), justly famous for his distinction between negative and positive freedom, could not resist, albeit in a footnote, the temptation of saying something about the measurement of freedom. Despite the interests and effort of philosophers, the most satisfactory and systematic contributions to a measure of freedom come from political scientists and economists, for a handful of reasons. First, social scientists are sensitive to governmental accountability and freedom provides an ideal variable on the basis of which to assess government performance. Of course, an assessment exercise requires a quantitative evaluation and suggests why social scientists were in a prominent position in the measurement of freedom.

Another reason that provided economists with a comparative advantage in the measurement of freedom is their search for wider normative foundations. Prescriptive analysis in economics is conducted exclusively in terms of a welfarist evaluative framework (e.g., Paretianism). A state of affairs is desirable to the extent that it satisfies as much as possible people's preferences. Since freedom delivers important moral information, it should not be overlooked in the assessment and should have a direct impact (i.e., unmediated by welfare) on the goodness of a state of affairs. Once again, for information about freedom to have moral content, we need some kind of quantitative assessment of its extent.

However, the most important reason has probably to do with the role of choice in the social sciences and society. In the next chapter, We shall dwell at length upon the central role that both the idea of choice and availability of choices enjoy, respectively, in contemporary economics and in modern capitalism. Here we want to underline the intimate connection that ties choice to freedom and the importance of having information about the extent of choice for assessing individual well-being. In the light of these considerations, the economists' comparative advantage in the measurement of freedom becomes evident.

All the available measures of freedom depend, in one way or another, upon choice (Bavetta and Navarra, 2004). By and large, we may distinguish two approaches to the measurement of freedom: one based on purely deductive reasoning, which we shall call *theoretical*; the other based on hard data, mainly drawn from official statistics, which we shall call *empirical*. The former approach establishes conditions (axioms) to say when a state of affairs dominates another in terms of the extent of freedom and, ultimately, derives freedom-ranking rules for states of affairs (Sen, 1977, 1987, 1988, 1991; Pattanaik and Xu, 1990; Sugden, 1998; Bavetta and Pergine, 2006). The conditions put forward by the axiomatic measures of freedom refer, for example, to the actual number of possibilities open for choice, the importance of each possibility to the end of the chooser's life, the value of access to opportunity vis-à-vis the level of preference satisfaction, and so on. The focus is here on the joint compatibility of different freedom conditions and on the interpretation of freedom that the interplay of those conditions makes possible.

The empirical approach starts from the consideration that freedom (economic freedom, in particular) depends upon the working of specific institutions (e.g., the rule of law, the protection of the fundamental rights of individuals, the extension of the state's intervention in the economy) whose characteristics vary greatly across countries. To assess how favorable those institutions are to the affirmation of freedom, the literature selected a set of variables that translate their characteristics in numerical values. An unweighed aggregation rule then delivers the final assessment on the degree of freedom that institutions guarantee to individuals in a given country. Since these indices target the conditions that make the affirmation of freedom in society possible, they can be used to improve upon policy and institutional design as well as to make governments accountable in terms of the enjoyment of economic freedom (Gwartney, Lawson, and Hall, 2011; Miller, Holmes, and Fuelner, 2012).

Although the difference between these two approaches looms large, ranging from their objectives to their methodology, they share a common element: Both attempt to construct a metric for measuring freedom whose foundations rest on the idea of choice. They do not endorse the same view; nonetheless, they rely on choice. The axiomatic measures of freedom move from the idea that the extent of choice signals a certain degree of freedom for the decision maker. This type of freedom grows if the extent of options expands and reduces if it contracts. In this approach, choice is important as it reflects possibility and, therefore, a space for action that is equated to freedom. On the other hand, the empirical perspective considers choice as an act resulting from the network of restrictions imposed on its accomplishment by the state. In other words, as institutions depart from what would be required by the ideal of limited government, people's choices change. The distortion imposed with respect to the counterfactual choices that would have been implemented under the ideal conditions is a measure of the economic freedom wasted by state intervention.

We take the connection between choice and freedom as the starting point of our analysis.[2] We think that in the analysis of this connection an important role, often overlooked in the literature, is played by the reasons for valuing choice. As our analysis endeavors to show, different reasons lead to different measures and allow a systematic comparison of the different approaches to the measurement of freedom. In particular, we suggest that choice is valuable for procedural reasons. A

---

[2] We are aware that some authors have expressed reservations on the soundness of this connection (Carter, 2004; Sugden, 2003). In the light of this book's aims and methodology, the most problematic objections are Sugden's. They are addressed at various stages, in chapters 2 and 3.

process of choice characterized by a wide array of alternatives among which to make one's choice is rich in the sense that requires, as Mill (1859) brilliantly argued more than a century ago, reference to one' own motives, values and aims and therefore contributes to developing autonomous behavior. If we are able to measure the richness of the deliberative process, we are also able to assess the extent of autonomy freedom each decision maker enjoys. As we shall argue at length across the chapters of this book, a measure of autonomy freedom is important for both theoretical and practical reasons. It provides useful, otherwise unavailable, information on the extent of individual freedom, it sheds new light on the justification of liberalism and the assessment of well-being, and it has far-reaching implications for policy and institutional design, with particular reference to social security and the size of the welfare state.

1.2 UNRESOLVED QUESTIONS AND THE BOOK'S AIMS

Once a brief outline of our project is delineated, we want to be more precise about the main contributions that our analysis may deliver, its novelty and consequences. A useful tool is offered by Table 1.1 where we place the two lines of research on the measurement of freedom, theoretical or empirical, in rows and the nature of the information used to measure the extent of freedom, objective or subjective, in columns. Four instances may then be distinguished.

Let us start by looking at the two cells located in the upper row. They both refer to the theoretical line of research and differ as far as the nature of the information about freedom is concerned. In the theoretical/objective cell, the use of objective information leads to measures where the extent of freedom depends upon the mere availability of opportunities. The larger the set of options a person may choose from, the wider his freedom since the extent of available opportunities signals a certain degree of freedom for the decision maker. Under these circumstances, the most well-known approaches to measure the extent of freedom are the simple cardinality ordering (SCO) proposed by Pattanaik and Xu (1990) and the preference ordering (PO) suggested by Sen (1988, 1993). With differences in emphasis and content, these two approaches share the view that the set of opportunities is an appropriate measure of freedom.

Table 1.1. *The State of the Art on the Measurement of Freedom*

		Nature of Information about Freedom	
		Objective	Subjective
Lines of Research	Theoretical	SCO & PO	AF
		↓	↓
	Empirical	Freedom indices	Subjective freedom

At the theoretical level, objective information to assess the extent of freedom is important, but it might not be satisfactory. This is especially the case if the measure of freedom should capture the procedural value of having choice, which is connected with the deliberative process that leads people to select a particular opportunity. Suppose we are interested in the effects of having choice upon the personal and moral development of an individual. Information about the available choices does not shed light upon the personal circumstances in which the chooser makes his or her own choices. We need, then, what we call *subjective information.*

Within the theoretical literature such information has been expressed in terms of the decision maker's preference rankings over the available opportunities. If we know what he might choose, depending on the preference ranking he selects, we may judge whether access to opportunity sets the conditions for his personal development. To the extent that such a process is germane to the construction of autonomy (individuality, as John Stuart Mill would say), subjective information delivers freedom orderings of states of affairs that assess the degree of autonomy freedom the decision maker enjoys. These measures are mainly due to the efforts of Sugden (1998, 2003), Bavetta and Guala (2003), and Bavetta and Peragine (2006). This branch of the literature originates a theoretical metric of subjective freedom, which is based on the Millian concept of autonomy (AF). In Table 1.1 the subjective/theoretical cell indicates this approach to the measurement of freedom.

The first goal of the book is to provide an account of how we ought to move from the left to the right column of the upper row. This implies a defense of the autonomy freedom measure as compared to other measurements of freedom existing in the literature.

Let us now move on to the empirical line of research by looking at the lower row in Table 1.1. The objective information about freedom informs the variety of indices that capture "distortion", that is, how much the working of specific institutions that affect choice (e.g., the rule of law, the tax system, financial regulations) distort it with respect to the baseline offered by the minimal state. Of course, the greater the distortion, the lower the degree of (economic) freedom. These measures – described in the empirical/objective cell – have been constructed by a number of organizations such as the United Nations, the Heritage Foundation, and the Fraser Institute. They assess the degree of negative freedom enjoyed in the economic domain around the world.

It is important to note that although the theoretical and empirical lines of research located in the column on the left-hand side of the table are both based upon choice and objective information, yet they do not cross-fertilize each other. The short circuit, denoted in the table by the dashed arrow crossing the two cells in the left column, makes it hard to ground the empirical measures – and, in turn, the results about the effect of (economic) freedom on institutional and economic performance – on a corresponding theoretical measure.

The same cannot be said if we consider the column on the right-hand side of the table. In this case, the theoretical measure of autonomy freedom is translated empirically in a subjective measure. Being subjective, such a measure can only be developed through surveys. We argue that the axiomatic measure of autonomy freedom proposed by Sugden (1998), Bavetta and Guala (2003), and Bavetta and Peragine (2006) finds an empirical counterpart in a particular question posed by the World Value Survey, an international database on norms and values collected at the individual level. Such an empirical measure constitutes our cornerstone in the assessment of the impact of autonomy freedom on social security and the optimal size of the welfare state.

Note that in Table 1.1 the arrow that connects the theoretical with the empirical line of research when the information about freedom is subjective is a continuous line (i.e., we hold and defend a theory that accounts for our empirical measure, which is grounded upon firm conceptual foundations). This is the second contribution of our book. It is important to stress that such a contribution is also of interest within the context of the expanding literature in economics on subjective testimony (e.g., on happiness and satisfaction) (Barrotta, 2008).

An empirical measure of freedom theoretically grounded on the well-established philosophical concept of individuality calls for a wide range of applications. In this book we focus on the effect that different degrees of autonomy freedom might have on both the individuals' preferences for redistribution and the size of the welfare state. This is the third contribution of this book. We start by the observation that people consider some sources of inequality justifiable and others unfair. Why does this happen? We find that one way of answering this question is autonomy freedom in decision making. We show that the higher the extent of autonomy freedom perceived by an individual, the larger her control over her choices and actions, the greater the probability that she supports the view that larger income differences are needed as incentives for individual effort. Conversely, the lower the extent of autonomy freedom perceived by an individual, the smaller her degree of control over her choices and actions, the higher the probability of supporting the view that incomes should be made more equal. If individual preferences for redistribution are significantly determined by the level of autonomy freedom, does this relationship affect the size of the welfare state? We examine this question by analyzing the determinants of social expenditure in OECD countries. We find that autonomy freedom shapes not only the individuals' preferences for redistribution but also the extent of welfare spending.

Another contribution is worth stressing. The measure of freedom that we construct is complementary, at the empirical level, to the measure of negative freedom. Complementarity derives from two sources. In the domain of empirical assessments, it springs from the different nature of the information used in the construction of the freedom metrics. In the domain of the theory of freedom, it derives from a more comprehensive understanding of negative freedom. In the standard view of classical liberalism, negative freedom is voluntary action, and it is sufficient to entail diversity. We do not hold such a statement as true. In fact, not all authors who believe in and have contributed to classical liberalism would subscribe to such a view. The complexity, illustrated by Milton Friedman (1962), of the relationship between economic (voluntary action) and political (diversity) freedom lends credibility to our skepticism. Under one circumstance, though, the claim that voluntary action entails diversity is strengthened. This is the case in which voluntary action is guided by autonomous behavior. The "operational enrichment" of the idea of negative freedom is the fourth contribution of this book. As we show in this book, the information that it delivers benefits both the positive and the normative side of issues in political economy.

Indeed, we go beyond mere complementarity and connect the basis of our empirical measure to a view of liberalism. This is the final contribution of this book. Though we do not press its consequences and envoy to further studies, we suggest that the concept of freedom captured by Millian autonomy seems particularly appropriate to solve some of the difficulties encountered by the classical – voluntary-action-based – version of liberalism without relinquishing its two most desirable features: protection of liberty and the minimal state. These difficulties are related to the fact that mere absence of impediments to the expression of one's will cannot guarantee the affirmation of freedom unless it is coupled with autonomous behavior. Consider, for example, social conflict. It would be too naive to think that its solution could be guaranteed by negative freedom since the rules of a free society might not be able by themselves to deliver the adjustments necessary to solve the conflict. We need something more than institutions: We need autonomous persons. They are likely to be able to come to terms with their fellow citizens; they are likely to be able to find arrangements that compose and harmonize divergent interests. In the absence of autonomy freedom, conflict might not be solved, at least at the private level. That would leave a space, a vacuum, that could, quite dangerously, be occupied by state intervention. Autonomy freedom makes more likely that, under the rules established by free institutions, people would look for private solutions to their conflicts. In this sense, autonomy freedom contributes to the affirmation of a well-ordered, open and free society, in association with nonintrusive rules and institutions. There is no analytical gain to extract from not considering the Millian concept of autonomy (and its extent) as a component of negative freedom, independent of voluntary action or noncoercive institutions.

1.3 AN OUTLINE OF THE STUDY

The book is structured in two parts. In the first we provide the theoretical and empirical tools necessary to develop the analysis deployed in the second part. More specifically, in Chapter 2 we lay down the theoretical foundations of freedom measurement. We point out that choice and its measurement are the core elements of a research endeavor known as the Freedom of Choice Literature. Within this framework, we discuss the reasons for valuing choice and assess the competing theoretical attempts for measuring the extent of choice that individuals enjoy. We dwell upon the competing merits of two axiomatic measures of freedom – the simple cardinality order and the preference ordering. We argue that even though the former proposes the idea that the larger the extent of options a decision maker may choose from, the larger his freedom of choice, the latter considers the individual's preference over the available options. In this second case, freedom of choice is greater where access to more preferred options is wider.

In Chapter 3 we establish the theoretical foundations of the notion and measurement of autonomy freedom. We point out that while SCO counts the number of options for the decision maker, but fails to account for individual preferences, PO suggests a solution to take into account individual preferences, but fails to address the procedural value of choice. Thus, we argue for a measure of freedom of choice grounded on the Millian notion of individuality. Consistent with the Millian framework, we construct and defend a theoretical metric of autonomy freedom according to which choice has a procedural value. Our measure of choice stresses the deliberative aspect of decision making and respects the liberal requirement of value-neutrality.

In Chapter 4 we propose the empirical counterpart of the theoretical measure of autonomy freedom based on the Millian concept of individuality. We point out that a particular question in the World Value Survey gauges how much autonomy freedom an individual enjoys. We, therefore, construct a unique dataset that blends consistently the theory and the empirics of autonomy freedom. Such a dataset covers approximately eighty countries that account for about 85 percent of the world population over a time span that goes from 1981 to 2004. We highlight that the empirical measure of autonomy freedom is generated through surveys conducted at the individual level. Thus, we stress that the empirical counterpart of the theoretical measure of autonomy freedom is captured in terms of individual perceptions rather than actual levels of autonomy freedom. We conclude the chapter by carrying out an empirical analysis to examine who the autonomous individuals are and what they think about politics, economics, religion, and society.

Once the notion of autonomy freedom is presented and its measurement accomplished, we move to the analysis of the consequences of autonomy freedom on the optimal size of the welfare state. In the second part of the book, we examine the effect that different levels of autonomy freedom have on the individual preferences for redistribution and on the size of the welfare state in OECD countries. In Chapter 5 we review the literature on the determinants of people's attitudes toward income inequality and their preferences for redistribution. We describe the effects of people's beliefs about social mobility on the distribution of income, analyze the consequences of fairness concerns on individual's attitudes toward inequality, and describe further economic, social, political and cultural motives that explain the cross-country heterogeneity in social expenditure.

In Chapter 6 we explain why individual freedom is an important determinant of people's preferences for income transfers. More specifically, we argue that individual attitudes toward inequality depend upon the extent of autonomy freedom one enjoys. We confirm our hypothesis using individual-level data on OECD countries. We find that individuals form their tastes for income transfers out of a principle of procedural fairness, which is based on the level of autonomy freedom they enjoy. The higher the level of autonomy freedom, the stronger the belief that one is in control of her choices and actions, and the greater the feeling that the achieved level of income depends on one's own choices and actions. This implies that whatever the economic status a person enjoys, she thinks that it is deserved. Therefore, for high autonomous individuals transfers are unjust prizes to the undeserving, no matter who the beneficiary is. The opposite holds for low autonomous individuals. The lower the level of autonomy freedom, the less likely the belief to be in control of one's choices, and the lower the feeling that the achieved level of income depends on one's choices and actions. Therefore, whatever the economic status, this is not deserved. Transfers should then be in place to compensate for unfairness in the income generation process, no matter who the recipient is.

In Chapter 7 we examine the relationship between autonomy freedom, preferences for redistribution, and actual welfare spending. We show that the greater the extent of autonomy freedom enjoyed by the population in a given country, the more people demand low levels of redistribution and the less the size of welfare spending. We argue that underneath this chain of causes and effects lies the principle of procedural fairness whereby redistributive policies are not aimed at reducing income inequality per se, but their goal is to correct unjust processes that determine economic success or failure in people's lives. Countries in which individuals believe that effort and merit are rewarded and that there is a chance to achieve economic success out of one's commitment and hard work are characterized by a low demand for income transfers. On the contrary, countries where individuals believe that economic conditions are more a matter of luck and connections and that people have little chance to achieve economic success in life out of their own effort and commitment display a high demand for redistribution. How fair the process of wealth formation is in people's eyes is therefore crucially dependent on the level of autonomy freedom they enjoy. The relationship between autonomy freedom and welfare spending allows us to construct a taxonomy of welfare systems in the OECD countries. We argue that for all these countries, with the only exception of Turkey and Japan, the principle of procedural fairness affects government redistributive policies.

Finally, Chapter 8 reviews the main conclusions of the book through the lenses of the procedural value of choice. Accordingly, all other measures of freedom, theoretical and empirical, are contrasted with autonomy freedom since they do not rely on the particular reason for valuing choice that we adopt. The picture that emerges helps to place our result in the literature. We compare it with both the standard negative freedom view embodied in the empirical measures of economic freedom and with the standard positive freedom view upheld by Sen with his capability and functionings approach. We also are in the position to sketch the normative consequences of our understanding of autonomy freedom and to place them in the bigger picture offered by a view of liberalism.

PART I

CONCEPTS AND TOOLS

2

Choice and Freedom

2.1 THE IMPORTANCE OF CHOICE

The role that choice plays in the analysis of individual behavior has recently become the object of novel attention for historical and conceptual reasons. These reasons are worth some brief considerations at the opening of our discussion of choice and freedom since they have to do with the importance that the fulfilment of autonomy has gained in contemporary life, fulfilment for which choice is fundamental.

The Changing Role of Choice: Facts

Since capitalism unbounded its strengths at the end of the eighteenth century, the enlargement of the extent of choice that it permits has always been pinpointed as both a constitutive feature of such a system of production and a prominent justification for its accomplishments. In the last few decades, the extent to which people can make choices and are aware of the choices they make increased dramatically. Since the days in which Henry Ford used to say that "people can have the Model T in any color – so long as it's black," capitalism overhauled people's lives by putting into the hands of individuals the possibility of shaping their own destinies in ways that were then unthinkable.

Such a momentous revolution involves all domains of our daily experience on the Earth – economic, social, and political. Witness what is happening with one of the most common domestic appliance: the TV set. Thanks to cable and satellite the amount of choice – channels and programs – at, literally, the finger of the consumer has grown exponentially allowing viewers to "talk" to their TV sets as they already do with their computers. The new television experience that is advancing will allow people to call up what they want when they want it. Channels and programs will become tailored to the tastes and wishes of each consumer, in the sense that control of what to watch is put in the hands of the final user, making choice central to the development of future strategies of the industry. As George Gilder, a technology guru, put it, back in 1994, "[e]rstwhile couch potatoes will no longer settle for a few score lowest-common-denominator programmes; they will range databases around the globe to pick out the first choice of materials. [...] The entire TV culture will give way to a radically different teleputer culture. The result will resemble the current arrays of thousands of specialized books and magazines far more than a few TV shows oriented to the morbid fears and prurient interests of a mass audience."[1]

Similar observations apply to other productive sectors and social domains. To respond to the increasingly competitive and international nature of the industry, car manufacturers have diversified their products: cars are nowadays sold with a surprisingly wide array of alternative combinations of gadgets to "personalize" each model to the customer's specific tastes and requirements. Despite widespread reductions in political participation and civic engagement (or, maybe, because of), political and civil organizations, in the form of parties, unions, environmental organizations, religious groups, local associations, etc., have adapted to a sophisticated demand for participation so as to occupy a previously unperceived (and probably even not available) array of niches in society that guarantees identification and the right of voice to an incredibly diverse set of people and instances.

Even the public sector is organizing its sluggish and convoluted bureaucratic machine in such a way as to grant choice, in school, in health, and in many other services provided to citizens. To respond to people's quest for "good service," public provision changed substantially, putting user's choice and competition at the forefront. And so did political rhetoric and aims. In a speech delivered at Guys and

---

[1] The quotation has been extracted from a survey published by *The Economist* on April 13, 2002, about the television industry with the appropriate title of "Power in Your Hand."

St Thomas' Hospital, London, on June 23, 2004, Tony Blair, the then British prime minister, put at the center of his concerns the need for improvements in public services and the importance of an entirely new design for the welfare state inherited by the British citizen from the previous century. In his words, the new welfare state should "base the service round the user" so as to guarantee "a personalised service with real choice, greater individual responsibility and high standards."[2]

Irrespective of which domain – economic, social, or political – we consider, the historical evolution of capitalism is therefore intimately connected to an increased amount of choice. This is undoubtedly a beneficial outcome of fiercer competition unleashed by the use of markets in the allocation of resources. But, at the same time, it is the consequence of the relentless individual search for a fuller realization of the self. Such a search is consigned, as we have seen, to our historical experience. But, it is not restricted to that particular experience as it underpins the evolution of the role of choice in the domain of ideas, too.

The Changing Role of Choice: Ideas

Choice, Capitalism, and Freedom

Milton Friedman is among the most prominent thinkers who envisaged a central role for choice in the capitalist system and interpreted it in terms of individual freedom.[3] In *Capitalism and Freedom*, Friedman argues – at an abstract level – that *competitive capitalism* (i.e.,

---

[2] Blair's speech is explicit about the centrality of choice:

In reality, I believe people do want choice, in public services as in other services. But anyway choice isn't an end in itself. It is one important mechanism to ensure that citizens can indeed secure good schools and health services in their communities. And choice matters as much within those institutions as between them: better choice of learning options for each pupil within secondary schools; better choice of access routes into the health service. Choice puts the levers in the hands of parents and patients so that they as citizens and consumers can be a driving force for improvement in their public services.

Besides its political value, Blair's speech highlights the importance of choice in the design of public policies. See Dowding and John (2009) and Le Grand (2003, 2007) for two interesting perspectives on this issue.

[3] Freidman (1962) and Friedman and Friedman (1980). In fact, Friedman views choice as determinant to the achievement of both economic and political freedom.

a society organized through voluntary exchange) is "a system of economic freedom and a necessary condition for political freedom" (p. 4).[4] Competitive capitalism guarantees economic freedom because its constitutive feature is voluntary exchange. It also fosters political freedom because competitive capitalism pulverizes decision making and, in so doing, facilitates limited concentration of political power.

Friedman's defense of competitive capitalism hinges upon its favorable effects on choice and, in turn, on economic and political freedom. He compares the decision process entailed by markets as opposed to political channels. The former permits the widest possibility for choice in the sense that it resembles, de facto, a system of perfectly proportional representation where each individual gets what she wants and might, ultimately, express in full her individuality. Political channels, on the contrary, rely upon a majoritarian decision process where those in the minority must submit. Submission necessarily entails a limitation to the full manifestation of the self since certain wants that people may entertain shall never be accomplished. Ultimately, then, market-like processes of decision making favor choice and therefore freedom lending support to competitive capitalism.

Beside their positive consequences on economic freedom, market-like processes of decision making might trigger favorable effects on political freedom since they dissolve power in society by "removing the organization of economic activity from the control of political authority" (Friedman, 1962, p. 15). Once again, as decision making is decentralized, choice is protected even in the political dimension, providing one further justification for competitive capitalism.

This is not all. According to Friedman, choice is not only the justification for competitive capitalism. It is also a manifestation of individual liberty. Consider the case of education. If people underinvest in education, Friedman the libertarian calls for government intervention aimed not at providing pupils with free education in state schools, but at giving parents the possibility to choose the school where to send their children by means of a voucher system. In so doing, Friedman makes choice a *value* that may be traded-off with negative freedom affirming, once

---

[4] It is interesting to note that competitive capitalism is merely necessary for political freedom, not sufficient. As we suggested in the opening chapter, a prominent motivation for the measure of freedom we develop in this book exploits Friedman's careful statement about the conditions for the affirmation of political freedom.

again, the intimate connection existing between choice and freedom and the central role that choice occupies in his view of capitalism.

Choice, Well-Being, and Freedom

Another prominent scholar whose work has been concerned with the role of choice is Amartya Sen. Though distant from Friedman's position, Sen gives an unprecedented role to choice and shares with the Chicago economist the idea that choice and freedom go hand in hand. Sen's argument pursues a different aim and follows a different path. Unattracted by a defense of capitalism, Sen attributes importance to choice since he endorses a normative perspective centered on the multifaceted dimension of a decision maker's well-being. According to Sen, a person's well-being cannot be exclusively evaluated on the basis of the degree of satisfaction delivered by her most preferred choice. An appropriate assessment of well-being should take account of the possibility that the decision maker has to select a particular alternative among those available.

The centrality of choice becomes apparent here in the double role of the outcome of a decision process *and* the fundamental component of the deliberative process. In the latter role, choice allows Sen to extend the assessment of well-being beyond the narrow boundaries of preference satisfaction where welfarism confined it. And since having choice is enjoying freedom,[5] it is hard to deny that it should count in the assessment of well-being as freedom is undoubtedly normatively valuable. Choice then let Sen ground his criticism of welfarism upon solid foundations and, ultimately, is instrumental to his Aristotelian approach that supports his pluralist and objective view of the good.

The close connection between freedom and choice is strengthened if one considers that a decision maker may value both the alternative she eventually chooses *and* the set from which such an alternative is selected (Sen, 1997). Following Sen (1988), imagine a person who reads daily *The Times* over other newspapers. If the government pretends

---

[5] Sen is explicit about the coincidence of choice and freedom. In Sen (1988), for example, referring to the set of possibilities open for choice to a decision maker, he writes that "The budget set may plausibly be seen as an expression of the substantive extent of the freedom of the consumer" (p. 271) and, later, presenting his view of positive freedom, he writes that "the positive characterization of freedom is not only coherent, it also corresponds closely to a person being actually free to choose" (p. 272).

that people should read *The Times* – it contains edulcorate reports on
its activities – she may decide not to read it (choose another newspaper)
or even not to read any morning paper at all. The example is interesting for two reasons. First, it confirms Sen's close association between
freedom and choice as considerations about freedom must be made
in connection with the decision process that leads a person to make
a given choice. Second, the example challenges *internal consistency*[6],
the standard assumption of rationality admitted within economics.

The challenge to internal consistency is another important route for
attributing a relevance to choice beyond standard economics. Though
not immediately relevant to our purposes, a brief description is worth-
while to understand how far-reaching are the consequences of a role
for choice in the standard framework of economic theory.

Internal consistency claims that if a decision maker chooses x when
the set $\{x,y\}$ is available, she cannot choose y when the set $\{x,y,z\}$
is available, unless her behavior is inconsistent (Sen, 1993a). This is
because economic theory characterizes rationality by requiring nothing more than "correspondence between different parts of a choice
function" (Sen, 2004, p. 122), invoking neither information about the
context in which a given choice is made, nor motivations. If we reject
an interpretation of rationality that reduces individuals to "rational
fools," the process of choice takes an altogether different role since it
allows to articulate the decision makers' motivations.

The role played by motivations is unveiled and surveyed by Sen
(1977, 1993a, 1997) with a wealth of arguments. The relevant point
here is that, if choice should not be interpreted as guided solely by self-
interest, then it must be related to the idea of responsibility. In turn,
responsibility is connected with how many choices a person has and
the circumstances of her choice. Invited to a party, a person identifies
the most comfortable chair but, moved by a concern for some elderly
people gathered there, hesitates to occupy it unless an imperious host
assigns it to her.

In an immediate sense responsibility is involved in this example
since, given the available options, information about the potential
choices makes our guest accountable. She may choose a certain option

---

[6] For an analysis of the idea of rationality as internal consistency, see Sen (1977, 1993a,
1997).

for different reasons. For example, she might think morally inappropriate to grab the best chair in the presence of elderly people; or she might follow some rules of etiquette that define what the proper behavior should be among her folks. In all these cases, responsibility takes shape because choice is available. The moral or social duties the decision maker expresses in making her definite choice would be at best meaningless if she had no alternatives among which to exercise her selection.

Whereas Friedman identified choice as the desirable fall out of competitive capitalism and gave importance to choice as reflection of freedom, Sen's interest on choice derives from his search for wider foundations for both rationality and normative analysis in economics. Whatever the reason, these two authors secure a novel perspective to choice in the realm of ideas.

Choice, Public Services, and Freedom

The examples and the arguments offered so far operate at an abstract level. Yet, choice is connected with the motivational structure at the policy level too, as it has been recently argued. Le Grand (2003, 2007) has vigorously (and convincingly) defended the beneficial consequences of the joint work of choice and competition in the provision of public goods and services. According to Le Grand, user choice and provider competition offer a better structure of incentives to service providers than any other institutional setting. When user choice and provider competition model actors' behavior, provision is more likely to deliver high-quality services efficiently, equitably, and responsively. This is because, in a Friedmanian spirit, if providers face adverse consequences if not chosen, then they will do their best to improve the quality of the service.

High-quality services, efficiency, equity and responsiveness are delivered by the fundamental role played by the fulfilment of autonomy that choice allows. Consider the principle of autonomy (i.e., people's entitlement to respect as deliberative and purposive agents capable of formulating their own life projects). If fulfilled, users shall be able to discriminate among service providers in their search for quality, imposing limits on the slackness of the latter's economic behavior. The principle works for providers, too: Service providers that are autonomous shall struggle to differentiate their products.

The novel perspective on choice in the economic, social, and political analysis, emphasizes the role of the deliberative process and the
information that it delivers for the analysis of freedom and its policy
and political consequences. In the light of such a perspective, we have
to answer a fundamental question: How could choice be measured?
We start in this chapter with a simple measure of choice and move to
more sophisticated approaches as we try to fix the drawbacks of the
simplest.

2.2 A SIMPLE MEASURE OF CHOICE

How to measure choice? The question lends itself to a simple answer: In
a world where possibilities are not displayed on a continuum, the most
immediate and, as we will see, provocative way of measuring choice
is merely counting the number of opportunities a decision maker may
access. Though intuitive and straightforward, such an answer carries
over far more technical and conceptual implications and difficulties
than one should reasonably expect.

The language for measuring choice needs not to be reinvented: it
has been developed in a recent field of social choice theory which
goes under the name of Freedom of Choice Literature (FCL). In the
last thirty years or so, FCL developed a framework to overcome the
welfarist straitjacket, which imposes preference satisfaction as the sole
criterion in the judgements of states of affairs.[7] We shall not provide
in these pages a review of such an important literature. Our interest in
FCL is more circumscribed: to compare its main theoretical measures
of choice so as to highlight the characteristics of the one we propose, on
whose foundations we develop the empirical rod of autonomy freedom
(Chapter 4) which is central to this book's argument.

---

[7] The Freedom of Choice Literature (FCL) originates from the contribution of
Suppes (1987), Sen (1988), and Pattanaik and Xu (1990). Since then, FCL has grown
in number of pages, content, and technical difficulty. An incomplete list of contributions should include: Alergi and Nieto (2001a, 2001b), Bavetta (2004), Bavetta and
Guala (2003), Bavetta and Peragine (2006), Bossert (1997), Bossert, Pattanaik, and Xu
(1994, 2003), Carter (1999), Gravel (1998), Jones and Sugden (1982), Klemisch-Alhert
(1993), Nehring and Puppe (2002), Oppenheim (2004), Pattanaik and Xu (1998, 2000a,
2000b), Puppe (1995, 1996), Romero Medina (2001), Sen (1991, 1993b), Sugden (1998,
2003, 2010), van Hees (2004). For a review of the Freedom of Choice Literature, see
van Hees (2000).

Consider a universe of opportunities. A measure of choice requires to develop a ranking of all possible combinations of these opportunities (opportunity set) in terms of the extent of choice offered. To put it in other words, the issue at hand is to provide conditions (axioms, in FCL's approach) that establish when an opportunity set provides greater possibility for choice than another. As van Hees (2000) says,

[t]he problem is to find a *procedure* which takes information about the various opportunity sets of an individual as its input and which produces on the basis of that information [...] a ranking describing how the various choice situations can be compared in terms of the [choice] they provide to the individual. (p. 107)

Interpreting "choice situations" as "states of affairs", the problem we have is identical to van Hees's.

The 'number-counting' answer to choice measurement has been embodied in the simple cardinality-based ordering introduced by Pattanaik and Xu (1990). SCO compares pairs of opportunity sets on the sole basis of the number of elements they contain. Sets that include a larger number of opportunities deliver greater choice than sets with fewer elements. SCO's intuition – as well as its many oddities – is not new: A nice counterpart has been created by Luis Borges's vivid imagination. In one of his famous short tales, *Ficciones*, the Argentinean writer describes a very peculiar character, Ireneo Funes, who, like a modern South American Pico della Mirandola, was endowed with a formidable memory:

Funes not only remembered every leaf on every tree of every wood, but even every one of the times he had perceived or imagined it. He determined to reduce all of his past experience to some seventy thousand recollections, which he would later define numerically. Two considerations dissuaded him: the thought that the task was interminable and the thought that it was useless. (Borges, 1974, p. 133)

As it will become apparent shortly, Borges's oneiric vision vividly delineates the characteristics, the merits, and the drawbacks of a cardinal measure of choice righteously unveiled, in a more rigorous fashion, by the formal structure of the ranking constructed by Pattanaik and Xu.

As a matter of fact, the cardinality rule that they propose is the product of the joint work of three basic axioms which, taken separately, do not seem to conflict with intuition, but once they are put together, generate a number of counterexamples.[8] The first axiom is as follows.

Axiom 2.1 *Indifference between no-choice situations (INS).*
Consider two elements, x and y in our universe of opportunities. If we arrange these two elements in as many singleton sets, {x} and {y}, they must offer the same degree of choice, namely none.

INS says that opportunity sets consisting of only one element (i.e., singleton sets) do not give any choice at all. The reason is simple: If there is only one alternative available, the decision maker is hardly in the position of making any choice. The intuition behind INS seems rock-solid. But, consider the informational role of the axiom. Indifference between no-choice situations restricts the relevant information in the assessment of choice to the mere availability of the option precluding any of the characteristics the opportunity may possess (good, bad, large, small, red, blue, etc.) from having a role in the assessment of the extent of choice.

The second axiom introduced by Pattanaik and Xu is concerned with the consequence of adding an element to a singleton set. It goes as follows.

Axiom 2.2 *Strict monotonicity (SM).*
Consider two elements, x and y in our universe of opportunities such that x is different from y. If we compare an opportunity set that contains both alternatives, {x,y}, with a set that contains just one of them, {x}, the former must offer strictly greater choice.

According to SM, having the possibility of accessing two alternatives delivers a strictly greater choice than having access to a single opportunity because in the former case the agent faces a genuine choice, which lacks in the latter. SM then appears to be a straightforward axiom which does not clash with our intuition. Note, though, the informational role it plays: Strict monotonicity precludes, once again, any characteristic of the alternatives to play a role in the assessment of choice as it suffices that the two alternatives be physically distinguishable.

---

[8] The fact that Pattanaik and Xu's measure generates many counterexamples, as we shall see later, attests the fruitfulness of their intuition and should not be read as a straightforward rejection, on our part, of their result, despite their own dissatisfaction with it.

Indifference between no-choice situations and strict monotonicity are simple axioms in the sense that they deal, at the most, with two options. To generalize the cardinality approach to a finite number of alternatives, Pattanaik and Xu need another axiom, Independence. The axiom goes as follows.

Axiom 2.3 *Independence (IND).*
Consider two opportunity sets, A and B and an opportunity x which belongs to the universe of opportunities but is neither in A nor in B. Suppose A offers at least as much choice as B. If we add x to both sets, then their relative ranking in terms of choice they offer shall not change.

IND is a slightly more complicated axiom. Suppose we know how to compare two opportunity sets on the basis of the extent of choice they offer. Then adding the same element to both sets does not affect the comparison. In other words, whether A or B offer greater choice is not changed by the availability of x, which is irrelevant, in terms of choice, to the ranking of A versus B. The intuition behind IND is again hardly objectionable: If we add the same alternative to two opportunity sets, why should they be valued differently in terms of freedom of choice? The problem is, though, that the informational requirement imposed by IND disregards the specific composition of each opportunity set, which, as we will see, may make a substantial difference to the assessment.

Given INS, SM, and IND, the simple cardinality-based ordering ranks the opportunity sets on the basis of the number of elements they contain, as the following theorem states.

Theorem 2.1 *Consider two opportunity sets, A and B. A offers at least as much choice as B if and only if it contains at least as many opportunities as B.*[9]

Pattanaik and Xu's is an important result. To start with, it provides a neat characterization of a measure of choice that is plausible and intuitive. It is intuitive because counting options is a straightforward method for assessing their quantity; it is plausible because it reflects an immediate interpretation of freedom in terms of availability of choices.

---

[9] The binary relation expressed in this theorem is transitive.

Moreover, SCO's neatness makes it a useful benchmark for the development and assessment of other measures of choice developed in the literature to which we shall turn in due course.

Yet, as Funes realized, behind the neatness of Pattanaik and Xu's result lie its limitations. To start with, the cardinal approach is "useless" and "interminable" because of its naive treatment of diversity. Moreover, it is unsuited to treat cases of dominance (i.e., to give a satisfactory response about the quantity of choice when comparisons should weight numerosity against preference over the available options). Finally, availability of choices, though plausible, is problematic as a measure of freedom, at least if one is concerned with autonomous behavior, as we are in this book. We shall take arms against SCO's two major difficulties, *diversity* and *dominance*, in the final section of this chapter and postpone our observations and criticisms on the view of freedom to the next chapter. To start with, we turn our attention to the reasons why choice should be valued.

2.3 THE VALUE OF CHOICE

As we will see throughout the book, an important question we should focuses on the reasons why choice is of value. Its importance springs from the fact that different answers leads to different measures (Jones and Sugden, 1982), that the entire endeavor of measuring choice may be read and assessed on the basis of the value of choice (Chapter 8) and that it is the particular answer we give that motivates the Millian foundations of both the theoretical and empirical measure we develop.

So, why is choice valuable? The question could be answered in many ways, as suggested, for example, by the detailed taxonomy offered by Carter (1999). For our own purposes, Carter's distinctions, though analytically subtle and valuable, are exceedingly sophisticated. We may be content with a simpler characterization of the value of choice, based upon three criteria: whether choice has procedural value and whether it has intrinsic or instrumental importance. Let us start with the latter.

The Intrinsic and Instrumental Value of Choice

Choice is *intrinsically valuable* if its value is independent of the value of the specific things one chooses to do. In other words, its value cannot be "completely reduced to any other value" (van Hees, 2000, p. 153). Under such a perspective on the value of choice, having the possibility to choose a certain alternative from a rich set of opportunities is valuable even if one would never make use of such a potential. A decision maker who enjoys choice would value choice – in some unspecified sense – even if the option that she selects would not change if her set of opportunities reduces to a singleton. This means that, independent of the value of the specific option that we choose (or could have chosen), having choice is of value. In the words of Nozick (1974), choice is valuable because the act of choosing from various options is good in itself, and having opportunities is necessary in order to speak of genuine choice. A chosen way of life is better, ceteris paribus, than an unchosen one. Choosing has, in this case, an intrinsic value, and having opportunities allows its realization.

If choice is not intrinsically valuable, then its value is *instrumental*. The instrumental value of choice arises when its importance depends on the value of the specific things one chooses. The most immediate case is preference for flexibility (Kreps, 1979), namely a preference for situations that provide a wide array of alternatives in the face of uncertainty over the structure of future preferences. Consider a simple example: making reservations at a restaurant. If restaurants differ only for the menu of meals that they serve, customers face a two-stage choice process in which they select a restaurant (first stage) for choosing a particular meal (second stage). So, having a wide range of options to choose from is instrumental to the satisfaction of individual preferences.

This is particularly important from a practical point of view if, for example, it is difficult to collect evidence on preferences to inform social policy evaluation or to make choices. One way to ensure that as many preferences as possible are satisfied is to provide as many opportunities as possible, and let individuals help themselves. Just what the instrumental value of choice would prescribe.

The intrinsic and instrumental view of the value of choice attribute importance to the availability of opportunities either because options are valuable per se or because they favor the achievement of a higher well-being as measured, in our example, in terms of preference satisfaction. But choice may be valued not for the options in themselves but for the procedures that their availability triggers.

The Procedural Value of Choice

The *procedural value* of choice emerges when the value attributed to choice depends on the deliberative process that it presupposes. This is a characteristic of choice that is not adequately emphasized, at least in the Freedom of Choice Literature. As we shall see, most rankings of choice do not take into account the procedural value of choice, despite its beneficial effects both at the interpretative level – it attributes a convincing meaning to choice in terms of freedom – and at the technical level – it solves the problems that SCO encounters.

As John Stuart Mill emphasized, having alternatives to choose from confronts the decision maker with a process of reflection and evaluation of her available courses of action. Such a process calls for her personal qualities such as "perception, judgment, discriminative feeling, mental activity, and even moral preference" (Mill, 1859, p. 122). By calling for people's personal and moral qualities, deliberative processes deliver a desirable outcome: They foster the moral and intellectual faculties of each decision maker and contribute to shaping a better person. This, in turn, is beneficial to society, at least if one is ready to assume that better communities are made by better people.

Examples abound. Consider the case forcefully made by Hayek (1960) who believes that the betterment of the human condition requires a process of trials and errors made possible by availability of choices. In this case, choice has a clear procedural value that, in the language of Bavetta and Guala (2003), coincides with the exercising *of* choice. The deliberative process allows individuals to think about what they do, to assess the correctness of their choices, and, ultimately, to improve upon them as time goes by, leading to a better human condition. Without choice, no such a process would be possible, jeopardizing the chances of positive evolution.

Yet, the deliberative process may be useful for another reason. Since it commits the personal and moral qualities of individuals, it leads people toward fuller expressions of their selves. In this case, the procedural value of choice encompasses Mill's celebrated exercising *for* choice.[10]

---

[10] The idea of choice as "exercising" has been introduced in the Freedom of Choice Literature by Sugden (1998); the distinction between the "exercising of" and the "exercising for" autonomy is made by Bavetta and Guala (2003).

In Mill's romantic view, the possibility of making choices is instrumental in the development of a person's *individuality*, – Mill's word for autonomy – since

a person whose desires and impulses are his own – are the expression of his own nature, as it has been developed and modified by his own culture – is said to have character. One whose desires and impulses are not his own, has no character, no more than a steam-engine has a character. (Mill, 1859, p. 124)

Whatever the perspective we embrace – exercising *of* or exercising *for* choice – the procedural value of choice is functional to autonomy (Bavetta and Guala, 2003) and delivers significantly favorable consequences for the assessment of the entire choice measurement project.

2.4 CHOICE AND FREEDOM

One reason why the extent of choice provides a valuable information – which we rather consider separately from the reasons why it is valuable – is that having choice can be interpreted in terms of freedom. This is because choice reflects a certain degree of freedom for the decision maker which is impaired if its extent contracts, even if the most preferred option remains available. If that is the case, the measurement of choice project becomes far richer: From a measure of the extent of choice, we may infer information about the degree of freedom enjoyed by individuals and avail ourselves of an analytical framework where the notion of freedom may be articulated, qualitatively and quantitatively.

Consider an example. If the extent of choice is measured on the basis of a purely cardinal ordering, as Pattanaik and Xu (1990) suggest, then freedom becomes mere availability of choices: A person is free if she may access a large number of alternatives. But, looking at the other side of the medal, rejecting the cardinal rule means rejecting the idea that freedom may be interpreted as availability of choices. The choice measurement literature becomes then a battle ground for different conceptions of freedom. This perspective is hard to disavow and, at the same time, too juicy not to exploit.

The issue is even more attractive since the relationship between choice and freedom intersects with the reasons why choice is of value. Consider again the above example. The cardinality rule says that the only relevant information in the assessment of the extent of choice should be the number of available opportunities. This is compatible with attributing intrinsic value to choice. Having choice is important and independent of the specific things one chooses. After all, it is not by chance that the characteristics of each opportunity do not matter in the simple cardinality ordering. It follows that, besides discussing its implications in terms of freedom, criticisms to the cardinality ordering may be conducted in the light of the reasons why one ought to attribute value to choice. For example, if the value of choice is procedural, then choice measurement should not depend on physical quantities only, but on information about the impact of choice on the expression and development of the decision maker's individuality. From a claim on the value of choice, we then derive some conclusions about the defensible conception of freedom and, ultimately, about how choice should be measured.

Finally, choice provides valuable information for the assessment of well-being. Such an information carries over a content that, unlike traditional normative economics, we would not like to forego. This is because, as Pattanaik and Xu (1990) suggest, to pick up a^* out of a state of affairs A, which contains other possibilities, is not the same as to be forced to get it from a state B where a^* is the only available option, irrespective of which option the consumer considers as the best. Assigning an informational role to choice in the assessment of well-being contributes to reject monist interpretations of the good: an issue tangential and yet substantive for our research endeavor.

2.5 DIFFICULTIES

Our toolbox is now complete: We are in the position to argue in favor of a particular measure of choice on the basis of adherence to a view of freedom and a view of the value of choice. To move forward in this direction, we start with the main criticisms, *similarity* and *dominance*, moved to our benchmark, the cardinality approach. We shall then be in the position of reviewing the alternative suggestions developed in the literature to respond to SCO's drawbacks and to pave the way to a ranking of opportunities where choice has a procedural value and freedom coincides with autonomy in the Millian sense.

Similarity

Intuition suggests that the major concern with a measure of choice should be with the similarity of opportunities and that any algorithm that we may consider as satisfactory should be able to handle it. In other words, we would like that our ranking could be so intelligent – or at least so flexible – as to account for the fact that some courses of action (or choices) are so similar as not to offer an appreciable mutually exclusive alternative (e.g., soft drink cans that differ for the bar-code only). The cardinality approach badly misses the target: It fails to take into proper account similarity because of its independence axiom.

Recall the axiom's informational role: IND makes sure that removing the same alternative from two choice situations does not alter their ranking in terms of choice. As a typical independence axiom in social choice theory, IND sterilizes the (choice) judgment from the context in which this is made, imposing that any information about the specific composition of each opportunity set should be disregarded in the construction of the ranking.

Pattanaik and Xu (1990) provides a simple but effective example of the pertinacity of IND. Suppose Mary is considering traveling and that she may do so either by train or in a blue car. Since she is facing two singleton sets, SCO concludes that the amount of choice available is the same (none) in both cases. Now, imagine that, for reasons we do not need to be concerned with, she is also given the possibility of traveling in a red car identical in all respects to the blue one. The independence axiom makes sure that the ranking of the two opportunity sets is unaltered, but it cannot prevent our intuition from considering the two circumstances as substantially different. In the former case, she was actually facing two opportunity sets that, inasmuch as they provide her with no choice, had, pretty reasonably, the same rank. In the latter, the opportunity set that gives her the possibility of traveling by train or by red car delivers a genuine choice, whereas the same cannot be said of the set made up of the two cars. The conclusion imposed by the iron fist of independence may contrast with intuition generating then a first, serious, objection to pure cardinality.

Needless to say, scholars rushed to redress the situation so as to give cardinality another chance. To this end, they had to relinquish the neat distinctions displayed by Funes's formidable memory and to allow for some kind of general classification of "types" of opportunity. Bavetta and Del Seta (2001), for example, introduce equivalence classes by approximating opportunity sets from inside (*inner approximation*) and outside (*outer approximation*) and allow the equivalence classes to capture different "types" of opportunity; they then derive a cardinality of the equivalence classes as a measure of choice. Klemisch-Alhert (1993) proposes a more technically ingenuous device: She shapes the mathematical description of opportunity sets in an n-dimensional space and claims that the extent of choice delivered by a given set depends upon the convex hull of that set: the larger the convex hull, the wider the choice.

Unfortunately, whatever the mathematical ingenuity displayed to solve the issue, difficulties remain. Equivalence classes are appealing as they retain the best features of cardinality without making the analysis too complicated. Yet, they merely shift the problem ahead since they are unable to account for the different degree to which alternatives differ from each other. This hits the exact limit of cardinal rankings: They consider diversity as a binary variable overlooking the fact that it may instead be a matter of quantity rather than substance. For example, on many accounts it would be intuitively appealing to say that a blue car differs less from a red bus than a red bus does from a glass of red wine, opening the flank of equivalence classes to the same criticisms pointed at pure cardinality. Following equivalence classes rankings, the opportunity set {blue car, red bus} gives the same [choice] as {blue car, red wine}; yet intuition may still disagree. As to n-dimensional descriptions of opportunity sets, they are no panacea as "they take the degree of diversity within a set to be *identical* to the degree of freedom of choice offered by the set" (Dowding and van Hees, 2009, p. 378).

The "similarity blow" poses a serious challenge to cardinality. Since escape paths are precluded, we should ask what are we missing and whether what we are going to miss is in fact of great value to us. Or, to put it differently, our concerns should focus on the concept of freedom supported by cardinality and whether we should mourn it once we reject a purely cardinal order.

What the joint work of INS, SM, and IND delivers is an important result with far-reaching implications: Choice measurement should be based on value-free assessments of the courses of action open to a decision maker. The radical version of the cardinality project formalized by SCO cuts short any possibility of dealing with the value a decision maker may attach to each opportunity by ruling it out of the picture since its very inception. Nowhere, in the ranking proposed by Pattanaik and Xu, does information about preferences play any role in the construction of the assessment. This conclusion is reinforced by SCO's appeal to the intrinsic value of choice that claims that having choice is valuable irrespective of the importance or preference we may attach to each available alternative.

The point we want to make is that if availability of choices is intrinsically valuable, then the similarity blow is unsurmountable. Why should we value access to an overabundance of identical (or very similar) opportunities that encumber our personal self of useless possibilities? Even Funes would agree with this conclusion granted that, at some point in his life, he decided not to reduce his past experiences to a numbered set of recollections because the task was *useless*. If, on the contrary, choice is valuable for procedural reasons, then diversity contributes to the decision maker's deliberative process and to the exercise and development of an autonomous personality. Such a contribution displays its effects even in the case in which personal qualities develop in a world of similar possibilities.

The diversity issue then provides us with good reasons for keeping some distance from the radical cardinal approach but not, in our opinion, for rejecting the cardinal project for the measurement of choice, for two reasons. First, with some modifications (whose details we shall unveil later) with respect to the simple cardinality version, value-free measures of choice are, in our view, appealing. Second, putting the emphasis on the contribution to the exercise and development of an autonomous personality, value-free measures of choice may overcome the similarity blow.

Dominance

Like similarity, the dominance problem is highlighted by intuition: Some options are too inferior to represent a real choice and, as such, should not be counted. Also like similarity, the dominance objection to cardinality has to do with advancing a particular conception of freedom. Authors who criticized the cardinality project for its insensitiveness to the dominance problem do so because they dislike the idea that choice measurement should be value-free.

The "dominance" objection has been introduced by Sen (1991) and carried over by many scholars attracted by the idea that choice measurement should be value-laden and, in particular, should be based on information about preferences. Reduced to the bone, the dominance objection claims that the extent to which people have choice depends upon whether they may access options or courses of action that are in some sense appealing to them. In terms familiar to economists, they require access to preferred opportunities. Whereas the blame for the similarity blow falls entirely upon independence, SCO's failure to account for dominance and, ultimately, to distinguish alternatives on the basis of individual's preference, is attributable to the indifference between no-choice situations axiom.

According to INS, singleton sets must be ranked equally in terms of choice, irrespective of any characteristic that the option they offer possesses. In particular, how the chooser regards the relative merits of the alternative contained in each opportunity set in terms of preference has nothing to do with their ranking. Following Sen (1991), suppose that a person has a single option to go back home from the office: to hop on one leg (set *A*) or to walk properly all the way (set *B*). How could the former set ever provide him with the same amount of freedom as the latter once we acknowledge – could we deny that? – that its element is dominated in terms of preference by the opportunity contained in the latter? Stretching this logic to its immediate consequences,

[t]he evaluation of the freedom I enjoy from a certain menu must depend to a crucial extent on how I value the elements included in that menu. Any plausible axiomatic structure in the comparison of the extent of freedom would have to take some note of the person's preferences. (Sen, 1991, p. 22)

So, for example, suppose an agent confronts two opportunity sets. The first contains three ways of living that she regards as good, wonderful, and fantastic, whereas the second offers three further ways of living that she considers as bad, terrible, and awful. In Sen's view, the first set offers wider freedom to the agent.

Sen's message goes straight to the point: Choice should not be measured in a value-free environment, as the pure cardinality approach suggests. And since Sen admits a plurality of values without committing himself to a ranking, he allows people to find out their own views of the good by looking at their own preferences. In the light of his more articulated requirements for the assessment of the extent of choice, Sen introduces a measure that combines two principles: a purely quantitative one that he finds convenient to link to cardinality; a value-laden one that considers how options are ranked in terms of the chooser's preference relation. One' way, of course not the sole way, of ranking states of affairs in terms of choice is crystalized in the following sufficient condition:

Axiom 2.4 *Set-dominance axiom.*
Consider two opportunity sets, A and B such that A's cardinality is at least as large as B's and all its options are weakly preferred to their correspondent in B. Then A offers at least as much choice as B.

Axiom 2.4 is a sufficient (though not necessary) condition for claiming that *A* dominates *B* in terms of choice. It is sufficient since, once values have been accounted for, having more of those options that satisfy the chooser's values should deliver wider choice. It is not a necessary condition since *A* may dominate *B* in terms of choice even if the set-dominance axiom is not satisfied. This is because the evaluation of the extent of choice depends on how the two principles (cardinality and values) are jointly combined, and there is no unique way of hammering out the combination. Once we take into account the value the decision maker attaches to having access to a given option, there may be cases in which this value prevails as a choice-ranking criterion, even with respect to the cardinality criterion, namely to availability of choices. A formal translation of these considerations is provided by the following necessary condition.

Axiom 2.5 *Necessary condition for weak set-dominance.*
Consider two opportunity sets, A and B, and an option x that belongs to A such that it dominates, in terms of preference, all alternatives contained in B. Then A offers at least as much choice as B.

While the dominance issue poses serious problems to the cardinality project, the solution proposed by Sen carries difficulties of its own. Consider the sufficient condition first. Following Sugden (1998), assume that a person is indifferent between jogging for 15 minutes or for 20 minutes. He faces then two opportunity sets: $A = \{15\}$ and $B = \{20\}$. Now consider the case where he would be given another option (i.e., jogging for just 15 minutes and 01 second). His opportunity sets become: $A = \{15, 15:01\}$ and $B = \{20, 15:01\}$. Because of Sen's sufficient condition, the set A should be indifferent in terms of choice to the set B, despite the fact that the latter presents a genuine choice. Sen's approach seems unable to account for diversity, just as pure cardinality. This is unsurprising. Sen's use of preference is tantamount to the construction of partitions of the opportunity set and, as in the case of equivalence classes, merely shifts the difficulty ahead.

Another problem hits Sen's necessary condition. Stretched to its limit, it says that an opportunity set may dominate another in terms of choice if it contains the most preferred element, irrespective of any other consideration. But then what would be the difference with using the indirect utility ranking?[11] As Bavetta and Guala (2003) put it, if choice should be considered no more than the "underlaborer" of preference satisfaction, it would be hard to make full sense of the process of choice entailed by the possibility of selecting a given outcome from a sufficiently rich set of opportunities.

This suggests that Sen's attempt to solve SCO's difficulties via the introduction of preferences creates more problems than it solves. The point is, once again, with the reasons why choice should be of value. As we will show in the next chapter, if we accept the procedural value of choice, the difficulties fade away (Bavetta and Guala, 2009).

---

[11] Note that a similar objection could also be moved to the preference for flexibility approach and, consequently, to the instrumental value of choice.

3

Measuring Autonomy Freedom

3.1 A SHIFT IN PERSPECTIVE

The previous chapter suggested that attributing procedural value to choice heals the cardinality ranking's maladies. Though this would be a perfectly acceptable motivation for embracing the procedural perspective, we shall illustrate in this chapter that, in fact, there are other, more pregnant, reasons that invite us to opt out of the intrinsic and the instrumental values of choice for the procedural. They have to do with the interpretation of freedom involved by the procedural view of the value of choice and with the readiness with which the ranking we construct under this perspective on the value of choice lends itself to empirically meaningful applications. While the applications are the subject matter of the next chapter, the interpretation of freedom called in by a procedural view of the value of choice and the possibility to overcome the difficulties experienced by the cardinality rule are the concern of the pages that follow.

To adopt the procedural value of choice entails a substantial shift in perspective that requires some preparatory work. This is because the aim of the measurement exercise is to gauge the decision maker's *autonomy freedom*. None of the rankings introduced so far make any attempt at assessing the extent of autonomous behavior (or autonomy freedom), so the analytical framework where our argument has to be deployed must be different in the sense that it must assess the richness of the decision maker's deliberative process.

It is important to note from the outset that, though we use preferences in the measurement of choice, our utilization substantially differs from Sen's. The difference is the consequence of the procedural framework in which we work. In such a framework, information about the value of the specific thing that the decision maker may do is not of interest. On the contrary, the role of preferences is to convey information about the process that leads autonomous persons to select a given opportunity. As we will show, this task is accomplished by means of *potential preferences*. But, we distance ourselves from Sen in another respect, too: while we accommodate preferences in our ranking, we shall not do so to support, in any way, a value-laden measure of choice. This is evident from the axiomatic structure of our ranking of autonomy freedom which is based upon an "adjusted" cardinal rule.

The measurement of choice in a procedural framework has been recently subjected to a fundamental criticism: It aims high – to provide a quantitative assessment of the Millian notion of autonomy – but achieves less since no such measure may be constructed (Sugden, 2003, 2010). We cannot overlook this criticism. Yet, we suggest that, within limits, it makes sense to measure choice in a procedural framework and to extract policy prescriptions from the ensuing measure.

3.2 CHOICE, DELIBERATION, AND AUTONOMY

It is hard to underestimate the fascination exercised by the concept of autonomy, among philosophers and political theorists and the depth and width of the debate that its allure generated. For our own purposes, a person is autonomous if she has choices and if what she chooses can be accounted for on the basis of a deliberative process where she shapes her preferences over the available alternatives. In the face of the huge interest that the notion of autonomy attracts, our interpretation might appear quite narrow; nonetheless, it claims prestigious origins.

Writing in a period of strict moral customs imposed by social conformism – Victorian England – John Stuart Mill's apology of choice and freedom takes the form of a plea for individuality and eccentricity, and of a vigorous critique of social uniformity.

In our times, from the highest class of society down to the lowest, everyone lives as under the eye of a hostile and dreaded censorship. Not only in what concerns others, but in what concerns only themselves, the individual and the family do not ask themselves, what do I prefer? [...] They ask themselves, what is suitable to my position? What is usually done by persons of my station and pecuniary circumstances? [...] It does not occur to them to have any inclination except for what is customary. [...] [P]eculiarity of taste, eccentricity of conduct are shunned equally with crimes, until by dint of not following their own nature they have no nature to follow [...] Now is this, or is it not, the desirable condition of human nature? (Mill, 1859, p. 125)

Individuality in Mill's writing coincides with autonomy (Gray, 1996). It must be preserved and promoted in society for two reasons: First, because what constitutes a good life for a person may not coincide with the good life for another. Each of us may have to pursue a different lifestyle in order to exploit one's own capacities and talents. Secondly, because by allowing for experiments in lifestyle, we promote the discovery of new avenues, otherwise hardly accessible, that may be chosen in the future by other individuals. Perhaps there is a way of living that would be good, indeed better than the one currently pursued. But, if nobody is aware of its existence and viability, it shall never be chosen (or rejected) on the basis of one's own considered judgment. Letting someone else explore it, then, makes it sure that the range of opportunities open for choice in a society is enhanced.

Notice that, should one eventually decide not to pursue that mode of life, the decision to stick to her present habits would anyway be vindicated in the sense that a genuine decision must be based on the conscious, autonomous, evaluation of its pros and cons or on the comparison with alternative options. The existence of alternative options is thus necessary for autonomous choice and eccentricity (in the sense of experimenting with nonorthodox lifestyles) is crucial to make such alternative options available for choice.

Mill the "romantic" and Mill the "fallibilist" are both represented in these two arguments. We do not want to engage here in an exegetic analysis of Mill's various souls, but simply to translate these considerations in the context of the modern debate on the assessment of choice. Mill's point is that choice is valuable because it provides a space for the expression of individuality: Any attempt to measure the extent of choice must then be tailored so as to preserve that value.

None of the rankings reviewed so far may be of help. They are not constructed to accommodate the conscious evaluation of costs and benefits associated with each choice. They may reveal how many options are accessible or their value (preference) in the eyes of the decision maker, but are unsuitable to capture the essence of the Millian proposal: The deliberative process and the possibility to experiment with nonorthodox lifestyles. Pure option counting, *à-la* simple cardinality, does not even consider the space for deliberation in the development of its measure. Deliberation would require some concern with the way in which preferences are formed, or how individuals shape their own mind about alternative courses of action. But preferences have no citizenship within the simple cardinality ranking and the assessment takes place on the basis of the mere physical separateness of the available opportunities. In this sense, Pattanaik and Xu's measure is *a-deliberative*.

Sen's approach does not improve upon the picture. Despite its concern – for wrong reasons, as we suggested – with what people like and dislike, the preference relation used to construct the ranking of opportunity sets is exogenously given and does not provide any information that might be used to articulate the deliberative process. In this sense, Sen's measure is *post-deliberative*. A radical change of perspective must be undertaken if deliberation should have a voice in the measurement of choice.

By calling for an individual's personal and moral qualities – discernment, judgment, firmness, and so on – that separate the persons who are said to have character from those who behave like a "steam-engine," the deliberative process becomes the space where autonomy develops and is fostered. So, if a metric of choice is sought after, this has to gauge the richness of the deliberative process. Where personal and moral qualities have to flock in numbers to untie the counterbalancing merits of different courses of action, there it is likely that the prospect for autonomous behavior and for its manifestation are far greater.

In the aseptic language of the Freedom of Choice Literature, the deliberative process is the process of analysis and evaluation of the available alternative courses of action that leads a decision maker to select the most preferred alternative. Deliberation has to move to the center of the stage: It must become the space where the enquiry is conducted since there choice gives its contribution to the development and exercise of autonomy. It follows that the extent of choice must be measured before the deliberative process is concluded.

Such a radical change is accomplished by shifting the analysis at the *predeliberation* stage (Wertheimer, 1992), namely by focusing on the availability of choices *before* the process that leads the decision maker to shape her own preferences over the available alternatives is completed. At the predeliberation stage of the process of choice, options do not present themselves already ranked in terms of the decision maker's *actual* preference relation. On the contrary, the process of preference formation is still to be accomplished and any given alternative course of action may potentially be considered as the best one, depending on which actual preference relation the chooser will end up with upholding. With the selection of the actual preference ranking the exercise of choice shall be completed.

3.3 POTENTIAL PREFERENCES

Definition and Interpretation

To embody the deliberative process in the measurement of choice we make use of information about preferences since the aim of the process of choice is to elicit a preference relation that orders the available courses of action. Among the measures of choice reviewed in the previous chapter, only Sen's relies upon information about preferences. Preferences suits his needs as they establish a partition of the available options. Any further opportunity provided to the decision maker affects her choice only if it does not belong to any of the classes in the partition, for it would otherwise be undistinguishable from the options that are already accessible (Sen, 1991). Our use of preferences is not dissimilar, but it should not be conflated with Sen's, for two reasons. First, because we depart from both his motivation for valuing choice and from his value-laden measure of freedom. Second, because Sen relies upon an exogenously given preference relation to attach value to the specific things that the decision maker chooses.

In our own framework – which builds upon Jones and Sugden (1982), Sugden (1998), and Bavetta and Guala (2003) – the aim is gauging choice at the pre-deliberation stage. We then have to admit a plurality of preference relations since the essence of the deliberative process lies in the selection of the preference relation that the decision maker shall use to elicit the chosen option. In simpler words, at the pre-deliberation stage, an individual faces a set of potential preferences and the deliberative process leads to the selection of the actual one among them.

A potential preference is a preference a decision maker might have had, even though it is not the actual preference that she reveals. Keith shows a preference for kangaroo sausages with respect to rib steaks. But he may also have had the opposite preference. Since both views may be revealed by Keith, they make up the set of his potential preferences. Potential preferences are useful for the assessment of choice at the predeliberation stage since they separate the metric of choice from the contingent factors that lead a person to prefer what she prefers. In so doing, they open the door to assessments of the range of choice based upon the extent to which the deliberative process contributes to autonomy.

The problem with potential preference is twofold. First, as Sugden (1998, 2003) suggests, they need to be interpreted.

A potential preference ordering is interpreted as a preference ordering that the relevant individual might adopt (or, viewing her choices ex post, one that she might have adopted). In interpreting "might" in this context, we take the individual's objective circumstances (age, sex, psychological makeup, health status, ethnic group, social class, family status, etc.) to be given but conceive of her preferences as unformed. Thus, a preference ordering counts as a member of the set of potential preferences if and only if it can be regarded as eligible, given the person's objective circumstances. (Sugden, 2003, p. 792)

The passage highlights the need for a definition of eligibility criteria: Which preference ranking should be included in the set of potential preferences out of the universe of all conceivable preferences over some alternatives?

Second, potential preferences require the definition of some criteria – "catering" criteria, in the words of Sugden – that allow to measure how much opportunity for choice a given opportunity set provides to a decision maker, in the light of her potential preferences. As Sugden (2003) writes, we have to "consider how effectively each opportunity set caters to this range of potential preferences" (p. 792).

In order to answer these questions, Sugden (1998, 2003) outlines two alternative interpretations of potential preferences. The first one follows what we may call the "objective-list approach". A preference ranking is eligible if the decision maker has a *good reason* to rank the available options in that particular way. Such a reason, independent of circumstantial elements such as one's actual preferences, is grounded on an objective theory of the good. So, for each rational theory of the good there exists a corresponding ranking of opportunities; the set of these rankings is the set of potential preferences for that agent.

For example, suppose that both leisure and achievement are good for human beings for reasons that have nothing to do with circumstantial or subjective elements. A decision maker who chooses leisure pursues an objectively good life by selecting options that she has (an objectively good) reason to value. It is admissible therefore that leisure dominates achievement in some potential preference rankings, and similarly for achievement. But, if achievement did not contribute to any dimension of human well-being – since, for example, what the agent is seeking to achieve is ethnic cleansing – then, according to the objective-list approach, the counterfactual preference for achievement should not be admitted in the set of potential preferences.

An alternative interpretation of potential preferences has been proposed by Sugden (1998) himself. Sugden is skeptical about the objectivist approach, even tempered in a pluralistic vein, and suggests that the selection of potential preferences should rather take place on the basis of a *sociological* criterion. Consider a group of individuals identified on the basis of some characteristics other than what they prefer (say, the middle-aged British men, to use Sugden's example). Although each individual possesses his own preference ordering, the latter may differ from person to person. Nevertheless, it is likely that, as these rankings are expressions of individuals sharing some common pool of characteristics, every person will consider each of them as an ordering that he may hold. The set of potential preferences is therefore composed by the actual preference relations of all individuals of a given reference class of people. As Sugden (1998) writes,

[t]he idea here is that if someone who is sufficiently like me in terms of non-preference characteristics has a particular preference ordering, then that preference ordering is to be regarded as one that I might have had. (p. 325)

Sugden's original defense of such an interpretation of potential preferences was grounded on the idea that it is "straightforward," "operational," and "neutral between different conceptions of the good" (Sugden, 1998, p. 326) – where the latter is to be glossed as "the various different conceptions which happen to be upheld by the members of the reference class."

3.4 MEASURING ECCENTRIC OPPORTUNITIES

The second problem with potential preferences – the "catering" criteria – is more complicated to handle. Upon reflection, the reader should not be surprised if neither the sociological nor the objective-list approach respect the value of eccentricity that informs Mill's notion of autonomy. As Sugden (2003) observes,

> it is a great virtue of Mill's account of opportunity that it is not constrained by current theories of the specific nature of well-being, and so provides space for individuals to make life choices which, according to received ideas, lack moral value. (p. 797)

That virtue is lost if potential preferences are defined in terms of normality or on the basis of an objective-list approach. This is because both eligibility criteria limit the admissible preference orderings. An objectivist account disregards all the value systems that run counter to established rational theories of the good. Eccentricity must be explicitly avoided when it does not conform to any objectively valid theory of the good life. In the sociological approach, the eligibility criterion limits the admissible preference orderings to those that are held by the relevant social class of people. But then, those options or lifestyles that would manifest eccentricity or reflect anticonformist judgments cannot bear on the quantitative assessment of freedom. As a consequence, freedom is better preserved by focusing on the defence of negative liberty, where anticonformist judgments have a right to citizenship, than by increasing the range of opportunities available to individuals, since such an increase comes necessarily at the expense of a person's freedom to explore new avenues in life.

The shortest way out would be to search for an alternative eligibility criterion unstained by the difficulties encountered by the normal or the objective-list approach. Yet, according to Sugden (2003), this path is barred since those difficulties are sufficiently general to make for an impossibility: There is no eligibility criterion that could lead to a measure of opportunity that captures the scope that a person has to develop and express her individuality. Or, to put it differently, it seems impossible to tell whether any future experiment in lifestyle will add anything valuable or even genuinely novel to our current stock of options, *before* the exploration itself has taken place. We want to peruse briefly Sugden's argument[1] and then ask ourselves if it jeopardizes our project.

In terms of a measure of choice eccentricity *à-la* Mill requires that individual explorations (which generate mysterious opportunities) lead to an outright increase of the extent of choice. But, if the decision maker does not know how it would be like to choose such mysterious opportunities, she can hardly figure out ex-ante where the option would fall in her preference rankings. Unexplored opportunities cannot then be distinguished from those already available and their addition (or elimination) does not affect the extent of choice. To bear upon a measure of choice the new option or way of life must not be genuinely original from any point of view (Bavetta and Guala, 2009).

How damaging is Sugden's impossibility claim for our project? Let us think about the nature of the potential damage: If no measure of choice that respects Millian autonomy can be implemented, the defense of liberalism cannot rely upon choice but only on negative freedom limiting the use of the measure of freedom we propose. Any attempt at enlarging the set of measures of freedom, though welcome, would lack the proper normative status to support freedom-enhancing policies since their only conceivable conceptual basis must be limited to negative freedom.

A closer inspection of Sugden's impossibility claim, however, reveals that it stems from conflating two aspects of autonomy freedom that might be kept (and it is convenient to keep) distinct: The exercising *of* autonomous choice and the exercising *for* the development of autonomy. Mill's experiments in lifestyle and his emphasis on eccentricity and originality play a role in the exercise for the development of an autonomous personality. Yet, the measure of choice that we propose in this book is not supposed to capture the "exercising for" dimension of autonomy, but the space in which the exercising of individuals' autonomous choice takes place. Within that domain not only the measurement of choice is meaningful; more importantly, the connection

---

[1] A comprehensive rendition of Sugden's position is available in Bavetta and Guala (2009) from which our argument draws.

between choice and autonomy so carefully crafted and vigorously argued for by John Stuart Mill can be assessed in quantitative terms.

The distinction between exercising *of* and *for* autonomy can be usefully proposed in terms of the duties of a government concerned with the maximization of choice.[2] Sugden's argument is based on the premise that governments ought to be able to predict the future preference rankings that will emerge from their citizens' experiments. If they could not, they would not be able to guarantee the affirmation of maximal eccentricity. In fact, Sugden's is an unduly ambitious requirement. We may imagine at least three goals that a policymaker might want to pursue: (1) to offer citizens the opportunity of exploring new lifestyles so as to enhance their own (and their fellow citizens') space of potential preferences; (2) to measure the space of opportunities (via potential preferences) after the citizens have engaged in such experiments; and (3) to implement policies that maximize citizens' capacity to make autonomous choices. Only the first goal must be pursued ex-ante, and we agree with Sugden's claim that it is best achieved by minimizing government interference and simply letting individuals do what they like. The second and third goals of a government, on the contrary, are pursued ex-post (after the space of meaningful options has been defined by the citizens) and require a measurement of opportunity precisely along the lines of the potential preferences approach.[3]

Imagine, for example, that a community of opera lovers has developed a preference for Italian *dolce canto*. Two theaters produce performances that fit the current tastes of the community, and the only characteristic that distinguishes the two theaters is the way the performance is conducted. For some time, all performances are classified in the same category and constitute a single, undistinguishable, option in the community of opera lovers. At some point, however – via a process of spontaneous imitation, perhaps – a certain subgroup of opera lovers begins to attend predominantly the performances produced by the theater that contracts conductors whose artistic vision is more faithful to the nineteenth-century opera tradition. As opera lovers become

---

[2] We are indebted to Francesco Guala for pointing out this important argument.

[3] This claim is consistent with the view held in this book that our measure of autonomy freedom is complementary to the measures of economic freedom and that a complete and satisfactory quantitative account of negative freedom requires information from both rods.

aware of this, the theater's performances begin to take on a new meaning, associated for example with social class or artistic perception. At this point two new categories – and hence two options in the community's opportunity space – have come into existence. A detail that was previously considered irrelevant is used to make a finer-grained distinction among opportunities than was previously possible. Whereas opera lovers previously had one option in their opportunity space (*dolce canto*), they now have two (*dolce canto* with alternative styles of conducting). The space of opportunities has been enriched in a way that no one could predict. Although this change in the opportunity set could not be predicted ex-ante, there is a sense in which the set can be measured ex-post. Moreover, comparisons can be made between the two situations – before and after invention of new meaningful categories.

It is at this stage that metrics of choice play a role. By requiring that we predict future preference rankings, Sugden is setting the bar far too high: It is not surprising that such unreasonably ambitious requirements cannot be fulfilled. But then Sugden's retreat toward a purely negative conception of freedom is too hasty: There are important tasks that require the measurement of autonomy freedom. The latter is useful when we are concerned with identifying the space in which autonomous choice can be exercised, in the "exercising of" sense that we have outlined before.

3.5 AWARENESS

What kind of eligibility criterion may we envisage in the measurement of the "exercising of" sense of autonomy once both the objective list and the sociological approach are rejected?

Recall that the problem with the objective-list and the sociological criteria is that they impose too many restrictions on the admissible potential preferences and therefore leave on their way options that are relevant in the construction of eccentricity and autonomy in the Millian sense. Such a problem derives from the fact that, as we suggested earlier, even in models of opportunity measurement where choice is of value for procedural reasons, (potential) preferences are used, as tools that create partitions among the available options, eliciting, in so doing, the *relevant* opportunities (i.e., those that contribute to the development of autonomy in the deliberative process).

There are two alternative ways of assessing how potential preferences cater – to use Sugden's language – to opportunity sets or, to put
it differently, to measure, how much choice a given opportunity set
provides, once the set of potential preferences is fixed. The first is to
use some kind of *unanimity* principles. The second is to use a purely
cardinal ranking, as we shall do in the next section.

Unanimity Principle

Unanimity principle is a class of axioms that single out the more relevant options in the opportunity set in light of the potential preference
rankings selected by the eligibility criterion. A typical unanimity principle, for example, stipulates that adding to a set A an option that is
dominated in all potential preference rankings by at least one element
that is already in A, does not lead to any increase in choice. Other interpretations state that adding an option that is at least as preferred as any
element in A leads to the creation of a situation where the individual
enjoys at least as much freedom as in A, and so on.[4]

Unanimity principles introduce some weighing of the options that
reduces the deliberative space by establishing that leading an extrava-
gant style of life could not be valuable – either because it is in contrast
with the fixed and objective list of values or because it collides with
what the majority of people would accept as a valuable style of life.

Suppose, to take an example introduced by Sen, that we have the
opportunity of choosing between walking out of prison and being shot
at dawn. Having the option of being beheaded at dawn does not add
anything to this opportunity set because the new option is dominated
by at least one of the available options. According to the objectivist
approach, even if it were admissible that some individuals might hold a
potential preference that can justify the betterness of being beheaded
over walking out of prison or being shot at dawn, the unanimity principle makes such an option irrelevant for the measurement of choice. So,
though being beheaded is part of the opportunity set, it does not contribute to deliberation, nor fosters the decision maker's autonomous
judgement.

---

[4] Other examples are provided in Jones and Sugden (1982) and in Pattanaik and Xu
(1998), among the others.

But, then it is possible to make the potential preference approach compatible with the "exercise of" autonomy in the Millian view of individuality by retaining the first step of the procedure – the identification of relevant options – and eliminating the second one – the weighting of the options. The idea is to use the potential preferences of individuals in order to identify the relevant options, while dropping axioms like unanimity that impose further structure on the metric of opportunity. The result, as we will show in the next section, is a metric that gives as much weight to the options that are considered most valuable, as to those that the members of the community consider crazy, just as a purely cardinal ranking would; but which, at the same time, provides some space for deliberation because the potential preference rankings offer the necessary information for the identification of the relevant opportunities.

This is what a metric based on potential preferences should capture in our view. Such a metric would be purely cardinal in the sense that it would avoid unanimity principles. It would give equal weight to each option that legitimately appears in the set of potential preferences of an individual. The set of potential preferences would effectively be constituted by a permutation of all the possible rankings that can be constructed using the eligible options available to the agent.[5] These options would be eligible if the individual is able to weigh its pros and cons – if she is *aware* of what it means or what it is like to choose that option or pursue that style of life. The value of exploring eccentric ways of life then becomes apparent: By practicing a certain lifestyle openly and publicly (these two conditions are particularly important in the Millian tradition), one not only learns what it is like to live in a certain fashion; more importantly, one shows to other individuals what a certain way of life implies, and thus contributes to enlarging the menu of options from which all members of the community can cater for the formation of their own preference rankings. The autonomous search for one's own individual way of life is therefore best served by making sure that the set of eligible options is as large as possible, consistently with the Millian plea for eccentricity and experiments in lifestyle.

---

[5] More details can be found in Bavetta and Peragine (2006).

Similarity and Dominance Again

The second way to assess how potential preferences cater to opportunity sets is cardinality. We measure autonomy freedom by means of an adjusted cardinal axiomatic structure that shall be introduced in the next section. To start with, we want to dispose of the two major difficulties the we encountered in the discussion of SCO: similarity and dominance.

Turning backward, one will undoubtedly notice that we started from a cardinal measure and ended with a cardinal measure. This might seem odd, but it is not. First, because the two cardinal measures differ significantly for the role they attribute to preferences. The simple cardinality approach works in an *a-deliberative* environment where choice is intrinsically significant and the notion of freedom that emerges is value-free access to opportunities. The adjusted cardinality we shall present in the next section, on the contrary, is constructed making use of preferences and assigning value to choice for procedural reasons. The notion of freedom that it upholds is autonomy freedom, in the Millian sense. The distance could not be more significant.

More importantly, though, we want to stress here that there is another sense in which our approach departs from and improves upon SCO: It does not suffer from the similarity and dominance problems. Let us start with the latter. Dominance problems have been traditionally solved through the introduction of unanimity principles. Our approach rejects such principles. But then how do we deal with dominance counterexamples? In order to answer, we need to go back to the fundamental motivations behind the potential preferences approach. Let us start from the thesis that access to opportunity is a necessary condition for the exercising of autonomous choice. This standpoint highlights the process rather than the welfare aspect of a measure of choice: Having more opportunities is valuable not because it leads to achieve what one prefers but because it is a precondition for genuine choice. The rejection of unanimity principles is entirely natural from this viewpoint: Unanimity is consistent with a welfaristic approach to the measurement of choice. Opportunities, in contrast, should be seen in our view as instrumental to the exercise of autonomy. Autonomy is concerned with the process of choice, rather than with its outcome. Of course, the addition of an option that is dominated according to our present preference ranking, or even according to the rankings of every member of society, does not change the likely outcome of deliberation. But adding the option changes the process, or the way in which the outcome is achieved. If one takes this view seriously, then dominance counterexamples simply cease to exist. As long as we are aware of what it means to be beheaded at dawn, and of the differences (if any) with the options that are already available, it makes sense to say that adding that option does enhance our opportunity set.

But, how about similarity problems? The difficulty with similarity is that it is impossible to tell whether any experiment in lifestyle would add anything valuable or even genuinely novel to our current stock of options, before the exploration itself has taken place:

> Of course we can always generate a list of apparently pointless ways in which a person can do what has never been done before. But originality in Mill's sense implies finding a new form of meaningful action. Such action cannot be publicly identified in advance, because their originality resides in meanings that have yet to be publicly perceived. (Sugden, 2003, p. 803)

The problem arises from the availability of opportunities that are mysterious for us. In such a case we have no idea ex-ante how we would rank the option in terms of preference, because we don't know "what it would be like" to choose it. Of course experimenting is precisely aimed at figuring out where that option would fall in our preference rankings, and three cases may be envisaged: The new option dominates some of the available ones, it is dominated by some, and/or it is indistinguishable from some (all) of them. The worrying case is the third one: If the new option cannot be distinguished from the options that are already available then, according to our approach, its addition (or elimination) does not affect the extent of choice that we enjoy. The new option or way of life, in other words, is not genuinely original from any point of view, as far as we can presently tell.

A first reaction is that this seems to be neither the most common nor the most relevant case among those that worry political philosophers. The latter are traditionally concerned about cases of options or styles of life that are not made available (or are even explicitly forbidden) because they are considered inferior to other morally more respectable or simply sociologically more normal options. Few political theorists seem to be worried about whether the life of a stylite is relevantly different from that of an anchorite, and hence whether both or only one of them should be made available to people. In similar cases, Mill is absolutely right: The best policy is to let individuals explore and experiment as much as they like, as long as their explorations do not harm anybody else. But this norm is easily and spontaneously implemented because if you (the government) do not have the faintest idea of whether an option is worse, better, or simply indistinguishable from the available ones, you will certainly not bother to impose any restriction or prohibition concerning that option.

The much more common and politically relevant case is the one where collective prejudice and/or legislation prescribe that certain options should not be made available because they are seen as morally abject or simply different from what is considered normal. This is where a liberal standpoint becomes relevant, by stating that the availability of new relevant options should always enlarge the opportunity set of individuals, regardless of how the options are ranked by the individuals in the community. Hence, for the exercise of autonomy, more opportunity is always better than less.

Armed with these conclusions, we may then move to our autonomy ranking.

3.6 AN AXIOMATIC MEASURE OF AUTONOMY FREEDOM

The foundations of a measure of autonomy freedom laid out in the previous sections invite us to introduce two major changes with respect to the simple cardinality rule. The first is concerned with the space where the measurement of choice should take place. Whereas the intrinsic and instrumental value of choice require no more than information about the available opportunities and the unique – and exogenously given – preference relation expressed by the decision maker, such an information is insufficient to assess the extent of choice when its value is procedural. The reason, explored at length before, is that information about what is available cannot describe the predeliberation stage of a choice (i.e., the environment where we want to give substance to the measurement of autonomy freedom). The solution is to make use of information about the potential preference relations that a person has over a set of available options. In other words, we propose a measure of autonomy freedom defined upon the combination of opportunities and potential preferences. With such information, we are in the position to assess the extent to which a decision maker may exercise her autonomous behavior.

The second shift with respect to the simple cardinality rule is concerned with the criterion used to attribute relevance to the addition of new options. The discussion on similarity and dominance carried out in the previous section highlights a novel element in the measurement exercise: All new entries in the opportunity set must count. They must count, though, for different reasons than in the case of simple cardinality. Then, the prescription was based on the mere physical distinguishability of the options. Here, it is imposed by the enrichment that new opportunities – even if dominated – deliver to the deliberative process.

On the basis of these two considerations, we propose a cardinal ranking rule that orders combinations of potential preferences and available opportunities in terms of the degree of autonomy that they give to a decision maker. Such a rule is uniquely determined by the joint operation of three axioms (Bavetta and Peragine, 2006). The first, similarly to what the simple cardinality prescribes, sets the baseline of autonomy measurement (i.e., the circumstances under which an individual enjoys no autonomy freedom).

Axiom 3.1 *Indifference between no-freedom situations (INF).*
Consider two combinations of opportunities and potential preferences over those opportunities held by two different persons. If when perusing potential preferences each person concludes that she would always select a single element – which may be different from person to person – then the two combinations of opportunities and potential preferences deliver no autonomy freedom to the decision makers.

Axiom INF shares the thrust of the *principle of no choice* introduced by Jones and Sugden (1982) and subsequently used by Pattanaik and Xu (1990). Though reasonable, the principle of no choice fails to detect lack of autonomy freedom since it makes no reference to the deliberative process. On the contrary, we claim that if two combinations of opportunities and potential preferences lead to as many circumstances in which decision makers have no choice, then the extent of autonomy freedom they offer is the same.

The next requirement imposes restrictions on the effect of adding (subtracting) an alternative to (from) a given opportunity set, over the degree of autonomy freedom. We have argued that no matter the quality of the option vis-à-vis those already available, its addition must affect the deliberative process, provided that the new option is ranked somewhere in the set of potential preferences of the decision maker. This would have been impossible – as Sugden explains – had the measure aimed at the assessment of the exercising *for* development of autonomy concept. But, once our measure of autonomy freedom pursues the less ambitious goal of assessing the exercising *of* autonomous choice, the impossibility disappears.

In particular, the idea is the following: In order to be autonomy freedom enhancing, a new option not only has to dominate the existing ones in terms of some preference ordering available to the individual; it also should not be as good as to make the choice problem trivial. Hence, the addition of x to the set $\{y\}$ is autonomy freedom enhancing if the following two conditions are satisfied. First, x is preferred to y by some potential preference ordering, which ensures that x may be chosen from the opportunity set $\{x,y\}$. Second, there exists another potential preference relation such that, if y belongs to the choice set of $\{x,y\}$, then it is not preference-wise dominated by x. We formulate this requirement in the next axiom.

Axiom 3.2 *Addition of relevant alternatives (ARA)*
Consider a combination of opportunities and potential preferences over those opportunities held by a decision maker and an option that does not belong to her opportunities. If the new alternative may be chosen on the basis of the decision maker's potential preferences, then it increases her extent of autonomy freedom.

Like the simple cardinality rule, our last property requires that, under certain circumstances, joining sets together does not alter their relative ranking in terms of autonomy freedom.

Axiom 3.3 *Composition (COM)*
Assume that two persons express potential preferences over four separate sets of opportunities (two sets for each person) and that, on the basis of those potential preferences, both persons may identify some preferred options in the available combinations of opportunities and

potential preferences over those opportunities. Then, joining together the two combinations each person faces does not alter their relative ranking in terms of autonomy freedom.

Composition is intuitively related to the independence axiom originally introduced in Suppes (1987) and to the composition property introduced in Sen (1991).

On the basis of these three axioms, we generate a unique order of combinations of opportunities and potential preferences over those opportunities based upon the cardinality of the preferred elements elicited by means of the potential preferences (Bavetta and Peragine, 2006). This rule is particularly attractive since it represents a measure of the "richness" of a decision maker's deliberative process and, therefore, of her autonomy freedom. Note that the rule is based upon cardinality to fulfill the requirement imposed by neutrality among the different opportunities – dominance is rejected. At the same time, unlike the simple cardinality rule, it makes space for deliberation since it uses information about what decision makers may prefer before the deliberative process is completed.

4

The Empirical Measure of Autonomy Freedom

4.1 INTRODUCTION

We have laid down a theoretical measure of choice grounded on the Millian notion of individuality (autonomy) together with a fully fledged set of justifications for upholding it. In this chapter, we want to move from the theoretical measure to its empirical counterpart. If successful, we would have a powerful tool for conducting an enquiry into the effects of autonomy freedom in society. A tool firmly grounded on an established literature and on an important liberal tradition.

But how to construct such an empirical measure? We cannot rely on objective data since they are not available at the individual level of analysis that our axiomatic framework requires. We have then to search for information at the subjective level; surveys are the only source of this information. Our opening considerations must then start with the survey question that we shall use to gauge the extent of autonomy freedom enjoyed by individuals. More specifically, we point out that the *A173 – How much freedom of choice and control –* question in the *World Value Survey* (WVS) database captures the degree of autonomy freedom people enjoy. As we will show, the question gives an indication of how much freedom of choice and control people perceive over the way their lives unfold. We shall argue at length that the information captured by the question proposed by the WVS is consistent with the theoretical measure developed in Chapter 3. In particular, by exploiting two established theories borrowed from cognitive functionalism

This chapter has been written in collaboration with Margherita Bottero and Dario Maimone Ansaldo Patti.

and social and personality psychology, we argue that the richness of the deliberative process assessed at the theoretical level leads to control at the empirical, yielding the correspondence of the two measures.

For the skeptical and the unbeliever, we corroborate our claim by means of an econometric exercise in which we demonstrate that choice and control are strongly correlated with another measure of control included in the WVS data collection. More specifically, individuals who enjoy greater choice and control are also those who believe that success in life is brought by effort and hard work, rather than luck and external circumstances.

Once the connection between the theoretical and empirical measure of autonomy is established, we are in the position of gathering information on the extent of autonomy freedom enjoyed at the individual level both within and across countries. Such a collection of data makes it possible to provide some descriptive statistics on the cross-country distribution of the level of autonomy freedom possessed by single individuals and to examine their demographic and socioeconomic characteristics as well as their opinions about the economy, religion, and society. We then carry out a statistical analysis to give operational content to our empirical measure of autonomy freedom and present some simple correlations that enrich the information provided by our empirical rod.

It is important to note from the outset that the empirical measure of autonomy freedom that is proposed in this book is captured by a survey conducted at the individual level. As such, individuals respond to question *A173* by revealing the extent of autonomy freedom they experience. Therefore, the empirical counterpart of the theoretical (axiomatic) measure of autonomy freedom described in Chapter 3 crystalizes individual perceptions. The fact that we deal with perceived rather than actual level of autonomy freedom enjoyed by single individuals is an inescapable obligation that derives from the characteristics of the axiomatic measure. Recall, as a matter of fact, that the theoretical measure of autonomy that we propose makes use of information about potential preferences, which is quintessentially subjective. Such a subjective element reflects a psychological facet that, at the empirical level, can only be captured through testimony that individuals reveal about the extent of autonomy freedom they believe to enjoy. Therefore, the Millian concept of individuality, axiomatically defined in Chapter 3, translates into data in terms of individual perceptions. In this book, when we refer to the empirical level of autonomy freedom an individual enjoys, we always mean the extent of autonomy freedom she perceives according to the response given in the WVS question.

4.2 OPTIONS, PREFERENCES, AND AUTONOMY FREEDOM

We are interested in an empirical measure that could capture the extent to which a person leads an autonomous life. The guidelines of the connection between the theory and the practice of a measure of autonomy freedom can be retrieved by comparing the following passage from Bavetta and Guala (2003) with the question in the *World Value Survey* from which we derive the empirical information about the level of autonomy freedom. Here is the passage:

[t]he main attraction of leading an autonomous life is procedural in character: autonomy provides a certain value to one's action by linking in a coherent fashion one's achievements with one's preferences, as part of a process of self-conscious creation. In the ideal autonomous life, what is achieved must have been chosen, what is chosen must have been preferred, and preferences must be "of one's own" (not borrowed, for example, or not hetero-directed). (p. 428)

Our empirical measure of autonomy freedom is constructed on the basis of the information, provided at the individual level, by a specific question administered in the WVS. The question we are going to exploit to measure autonomy freedom, *A173 – How much freedom of choice and control*, reads as follows:

Some people feel they have completely *free choice and control* over their life, while other people feel that what they do has no real effect on what happens to them. Please use a ten-point scale in which 1 means *none at all* and 10 means *a great deal* to indicate how much *freedom of choice and control* you have over the way your life turns out.

In pursuit of both passages' thrust, in this section we shall begin with linking consistently options, preferences, choice, and achievements. Later, we shall argue that the intimate connection that ties together options, preference formation, choice, and achievement in the theoretical measure of autonomy freedom blends nicely with the connection that puts together freedom of choice and control, in the empirical.

At the theoretical level, the Millian framework on the exercise of individuality (autonomy),[1] brilliantly deployed in the third chapter of *On Liberty*, allows us to establish an analytical connection between options, preference formation, choice, and achievement, (i.e., the actual making of a choice). According to the Millian notion of autonomy, decision makers must enjoy freedom of choice to exercise their autonomous behavior. Lacking options to choose from, it would be impossible to put in place any deliberative process. Note that, by establishing such a requirement, our approach departs from an account of choice that rests upon the unanimity principle since, in the latter case, a reduction in the extent of choice may coexist with greater individual freedom. Consider the following case, due to Jones and Sugden (1982). A person faces three possible states of health: x, good health; y, pain without disability; or z, disability without pain. Subscribing to unanimity principles could lead us to conclude that whereas the set $\{x, y, z\}$ offers no choice, the opportunity situation $\{y, z\}$ does.

At the same time, options allow for deliberation if counterfactual preferences can be shaped that generate motivated choices (i.e., choices that can be accounted for on the basis of the reasons for selecting a particular preference relation). In the procedural framework in which we work, freedom of choice and preferences are therefore necessary for autonomous behavior and for making choices that reflect the decision maker's autonomy freedom. Note also that both freedom of choice and preferences are compatible with a liberal view since they do not entail any substantive value of opportunity, as discussed at length in the previous chapter.

Finally, as far as the theoretical relationship between freedom of choice, preferences, and autonomy is concerned, the connection between potential preferences and choice triggers two psychological processes. First, it makes the decision maker more committed to the choice she undertakes because it closely mirrors her view of a good life and the direction in which she wants to steer the course of her life.

---

[1] Our use of the word "autonomy" has been questioned in seminars and personal conversations. Mill refers only to individuality. John Gray (1996) interprets Mill's individuality as autonomy, and here we follow his thrust. We do not claim that this is the only sense in which a person may be considered as autonomous. Nor do we deny that the sense in which we are using the word "autonomy" is interchangeable with, for example, "accountability" or "personal responsibility."

Second, it makes the decision maker readier to undertake a healthy process of outcome revision in the unfortunate – and yet possible – case in which she could not achieve what she prefers. If a person peruses her potential preferences before making her choice and carefully weighs the available courses of action on the basis of her personal and moral qualities, in the face of a failure, she is likely to ascertain her faults (e.g., lack of effort) and to stick to her chosen course of action, were a new opportunity opens for her. These considerations are worth bearing in mind, as we will see shortly, in view of the fact that our case on the relationship between choice and autonomy should extend to the empirical measure.

4.3 ACHIEVEMENT AND AUTONOMY FREEDOM

The theoretical framework establishes a connection between having opportunities, preference formation, and achievement (interpreted as the making of choices). Yet, *A173* interrogates people about the degree of control they retain over the course of their lives, namely, whether they achieve what they choose. Clearly achievement is used differently in the two frameworks. As a consequence, some further logical steps have to be undertaken to defend the consistency of WVS question *A173* with the theoretical framework in which we articulate the notion of autonomy freedom. We borrow these steps from two sources: a branch of cognitive functionalism, named *attribution theory*, explored by Weiner, Heckhausen, and Meyer (1972), among others, and from the concept known as the *locus of control*, developed within social and personality psychology, by Rotter (1954, 1990).

Attribution Theory

An autonomous person's deliberative process triggers two behavioral consequences. First, it makes the person more committed to the choice she eventually takes. This is due to the sense of identification that the decision maker develops between the actual choice that she makes and the direction she wants to impress to the course of her life. In other words, since an autonomous person's choice is likely to be connected with her view of the good, she is going to be committed to what she has chosen, ready to implement and, if necessary, defend her decision in the face of the innumerable adversities that characterize life. Second, the deliberative process of an autonomous person makes her accountable for the actions and behaviors that result out of her choices leading to firmer control over the way her life unfolds.

Suppose Marc is looking for a job. He faces a set containing two alternatives: work in his father's bookshop or trust his talent and undertake some interviews to get a job in the banking sector. Assume that in Marc's circle of friends the belief is widespread that success depends on effort and merit rather than family connections. If he is a heteronymous person, he may borrow his friends' preferences and decide to look for a job in the banking sector. This implies that, since the preference ranking that he adopts is not well thought through, changing friends he might also revise his deliberation concerning which route to follow in order to get a job. In general, since Marc is heteronimous, it is unlikely that he is deeply committed to the choice he makes since the underlying deliberative process has not called for his personal and moral qualities to bear upon his choice. On the contrary, suppose that in the same decision situation, Marc carefully gauges the pros and cons of the two ways he can follow to get a job. Eventually, he settles for applying to some interviews and tries his chances in the banking sector. Having taken a truly autonomous decision, he is likely to be more committed to his final choice because that is what mirrors the way he wants to determine the course of his life.

Apart from triggering a deeper commitment, a thorough deliberative process means that the decision maker is prepared to undertake a healthy process of outcome revision in the case in which he could not achieve what he aims at. Take again the career choice situation illustrated earlier. If Marc is heteronymous, he cannot make sense of why he applied for a job in the banking sector. Instead, let us consider the case in which Marc examined with due care his potential preferences over the available opportunities and eventually decided to look for a job in the banking sector. In the unfortunate circumstance of a failure in getting what he was aiming at, he would most likely be able to pin down his faults (lack of effort or determination, for instance) and be ready to stick to his preferred course of action were a new possibility for choice open to him.

The simple example we have described suggests that autonomous individuals enjoy, to a larger extent, commitment to the undertaken actions and readiness to go through a process of learning by doing. A branch of cognitive functionalism, named *attribution theory*, has shown that these two characteristics – commitment and learning by doing – make the individuals "high achievers" and are related to the feeling of exercising control on one's achievements (Weiner, Heckhausen, and Meyer, 1972). More specifically, a high achiever individual is more likely to experience control over the outcomes he chooses for himself. Weiner and Kukla (1970) run a sequence of experiments targeted to clarify the relation between the two previously mentioned characteristics of the deliberative process and achievement behavior. They conclude that

1) Individuals high in achievement motivation [...] tend to ascribe success to themselves, and hence experience greater reward for goal attainment. 2) Individuals high in achievement motivation persist longer given failure than those low in this motivational tendency because they are more likely to ascribe the failure to a lack of effort, and less likely to attribute a failure to a deficiency in ability. (p. 19)

Let us summarize what we have argued so far. We emphasized that autonomous individuals are committed to what they choose (commitment), ready to implement choices and defend them in the face of adversities (learning by doing). Attribution theory suggests that commitment and learning by doing are two characteristics shared by high achiever individuals. These individuals are those that believe that success and failure have to be ascribed to themselves. Therefore, they are those who think themselves to be in control of their own life. This implies that successful people are likely to think they are autonomous because they are high achievers (i.e., they are more in control of their lives).

For our purposes, therefore, attribution theory can be seen as one possible tool to bridge the gap between the notion of achievement pertaining to our theoretical interpretation of autonomy freedom and that referred to in the WVS question *A173* where explicit reference is made to "control." This is because it shows that there is evidence supporting the claim that autonomous agents are more likely to experience control over the outcomes in their lives and hence that high reported values in *A173* correctly indicate high levels of autonomy freedom. Thus, WVS question *A173* does assess the degree of autonomy freedom that the respondent enjoys.

Locus of Control

Social and personality psychology offers a particularly appropriate and useful concept that helps exploring the relationship people develop between choices and achievements. This concept, labeled *locus of control*, was initially proposed by Rotter (1954, 1990). Rotter distinguishes personality types on the basis of their belief upon the role of efforts and skills on achievements.

Those who attribute the outcomes of their actions to factors such as effort and skill are called "internals". On the contrary, those who attribute the outcomes of their actions to factors such as faith or destiny are called "externals". Internals and externals can be listed on a continuum according to their locus of control (i.e., their belief upon the extent of control they exert over their achievements). Thus, whenever a decision maker is an internal, she is also autonomous: She retains control over her achievements in the sense that they can be traced to her own choices.

In a recent paper, Verme (2009) uses the WVS variable *A173 – How much freedom of choice and control* as a proxy for freedom of choice and the locus of control. He shows that the two components of the question – freedom of choice and control – are clearly separated by the survey respondents. More specifically, he picks two variables that are expected to be insensitive to freedom of choice but sensitive to the locus of control, though in an opposite fashion, for internals and externals. Then, he regresses *A173* on the two variables as well as on some controls concluding that, in the eyes of respondents, freedom of choice and the locus of control are two separate components of *A173*.

This being the case, we may safely conclude that *A173* is a variable that incorporates the two elements of our interpretation of autonomy freedom: the availability of options (freedom of choice) and the awareness that choices are connected with achievements (the locus of control). Once again, WVS question *A173* assesses the degree of autonomy freedom that the respondent enjoys.

4.4 DOES AUTONOMY FREEDOM LEAD TO CONTROL?

For the skeptical and unbeliever, in this section we corroborate the claim that the notion of control in the theoretical and the empirical frameworks may be assimilated by demonstrating that autonomy freedom is strongly correlated with another measure of control included in the WVS database. More specifically, we show that individuals who enjoy freedom of choice and control are also those who believe that effort and hard work, instead of luck or connections, determine success in life.

The Data and the Empirical Model

We use data from the WVS database, which is designed to enable a cross-national, cross-cultural comparison of values and norms on a wide variety of topics and to monitor changes in values and attitudes across the globe. This data collection contains survey data from four waves carried out in 1981-1984, 1990–1993, 1994–1997, and 1999–2004. These survey responses have been integrated into one data-set to exploit the longitudinal dimension of the data. The survey is performed on nationally representative samples of approximately sixty countries that include 85 percent of the world's population distributed over a wide spectrum across a number of social and economic variables.

The empirical question we examine in this section is whether our measure of autonomy freedom explains control over life outcomes. To accomplish this task we need a variable to proxy the extent to which life outcomes are the result of individual decision making rather than the outcome of choices that escape from the individuals' control being originated by third party's will or by fate. To this purpose we select from the WVS database the variable *E40 – Hard work brings success –* which reads as follows:

How would you place your views on this scale? 1 means that you agree completely with the statement that, in the long run, *hard work brings a better life*. 10 means that you agree completely with the statement that, *hard work does not generally bring success which is more a matter of luck and connections*. If your views fall somewhere in between, you can choose any number in between.

Answers to *E40* show whether an individual is likely to be in control over the way his life turns out. Those who believe that effort and hard work bring a better living are more likely to take control over their lives. On the contrary, those who consider luck and connections as determinants of success in life, are more likely to display fatalistic attitudes about the way their life is expected to move ahead or lean on the contributions of others to advance the prospects of their existence. While the former individuals are in control of their life, the latter are not.

Since variable *E40* is a valid proxy for control, it can be used to evaluate the extent to which our measure of autonomy freedom explains control over life outcomes. To this end, we estimate the following ordered logit model:

$$Luck\_vs\_Work_{i,c,t}^s = \alpha AF_{i,c,t}^s + \beta Demg_{i,c,t}^s + \varepsilon_{i,c,t}^s \qquad (4.1)$$

where $Luck\_vs\_Work_{i,c,t}^s$ is our proxy for control of individual i in country c at time t. It measures the extent to which an individual believes that luck, instead of effort, brings success in life. The variable ranges from 1 (high control) to 10 (low control). *AF* indicates the level of autonomy freedom. It ranges from 1 (low autonomy freedom) to 10 (high autonomy freedom); *Demg* is a vector of control variables referring to the demographic characteristics of respondents including sex, age, marital status, education level, number of children and size of town; ε is the independent and identically distributed error term.

The superscript s in the equation indicates that in carrying out the empirical analysis we consider the full sample (in which case s = full sample) as well as different subsamples divided on the basis of the political orientation of the respondents (s = either left-wing or right-wing party supporters), their sex (s = male or female) and marital status (s = single or married), their religious beliefs (s = either Catholics or Muslims or Protestants) and the country where they live (s = individuals living either in OECD non-transition or OECD transition countries).

Before turning to the estimation, it is important to note that the data used in our regression analysis are drawn from a complex sample survey. The source of data is an important issue, since the observations included in the survey are selected through a random process. However, different observations have different probabilities of selection. These probabilities are approximated by specific weights, which are attached to each observation. Omitting those weights from the estimation may result in biased point estimates. Moreover, it should be also taken into consideration that observations are not usually sampled independently but as a group. Therefore, clustering observations is a necessary step, when dealing with survey data, since omitting this procedure may have consequences on standard error estimates and hypothesis testing. Another issue related to the use of survey data refers to the fact that clusters may be sampled separately. Therefore, in order to have more precise estimates of standard errors, we need to stratify observations. Generally speaking, if weighting, clustering, and stratification of the survey data are not carried out, it is unlikely that standard errors can be considered as correct, leading to erroneous hypothesis testing (Greene, 2007).

In order to overcome the problems pointed out so far, we estimate equation 4.1 using the sample weights included in the WVS database. Moreover, we cluster the observations according to the country where the interviews have been carried out. Finally, the data are stratified according to the year in which the interviews took place.

Table 4.1 displays some descriptive statistics of the variables used in our empirical investigation and the correlation matrix.

Estimation Results

In Table 4.2 we show the regression results for the baseline model. For our purposes, the most important finding is that individuals with higher levels of autonomy freedom are more likely to think that work, rather than luck or connections, brings a better living. Thus, in line with what argued in the previous sections of this study, autonomy freedom seems to be associated with greater control over life outcomes. It is relevant also to note that the effect of autonomy freedom is statistically significant even after the addition of the demographic controls (see column (b)). The results shown in Table 4.2, therefore, support the validity of the variable *A173 – Freedom of choice and control –* as a measure of the extent of autonomy freedom enjoyed by individuals. Finally, the statistics displayed in Table 4.2 also indicate that the probability of being in control increases for those individuals who are male, young, single, well-educated, employed and have numerous children.

To check the robustness of our findings, we perform some sensitivity analysis by partitioning our dataset on the basis of some demographic, political, and religious characteristics of the individuals included in our sample as well as on the basis of their countries of origin. Results are displayed in Tables 4.3–4.6. In columns (c) to (f) of Table 4.3,

Table 4.1. *Summary Statistics and Correlation Matrix*

	Variable	Obs	Mean	SD	Min	Max
1	Autonomy Freedom	108082	6.826622	2.272297	1	10
2	Effort vs Luck	53268	4.511827	2.702311	1	10
3	Gender	107957	1.526645	0.4992919	1	2
4	Age	106394	44.01837	16.63045	15	101
5	Number of Children	108082	1.864075	1.567609	0	8
6	Single	107711	0.1889408	0.3914634	0	1
7	Married	107711	0.6331851	0.4819376	0	1
8	Education	57342	1.829113	0.7571068	1	3
9	Full-time Employee	106393	0.4202062	0.4935942	0	1
10	Part-time Employee	106393	0.0793661	0.2703106	0	1
11	Self-Employee	106393	0.0675608	0.250992	0	1
12	Unemployed	106393	0.0508022	0.2195946	0	1
13	Income	89120	4.999764	2.533451	1	11
14	Size of Town	76674	4.69129	2.43502	1	9
15	Political Orientation	90048	5.509095	2.076797	1	10
16	Competition	86109	3.698719	2.397925	1	10
17	Trust	102937	1.640809	0.4797655	1	2
18	Catholic	82680	0.0171867	0.1299676	0	1
19	Protestant	82680	0.5292937	0.4991442	0	1
20	Muslim	82680	0.2944606	0.4558027	0	1

the sample of individuals under investigation in this study is split on the basis of demographic characteristics. We observe that no matter whether respondents are male or female, single or married, higher levels of autonomy freedom lead people to believe that work and effort do pay in life. Therefore, regardless of the demographic features of the respondents, autonomy freedom always significantly explains control over life outcomes. Regarding the demographic controls, even though gender does not matter as far as the higher probability that young individuals are in control of their lives, females only seem to be more in control if they are more educated and if employed. On the other hand, the probability of exercising a greater control over the way an

Table 4.1 (continued)

Variable		1	2	3	4	5	6	7	8	9	10	11	12	13	14	15	16	17	18	19	20
1	Autonomy Freedom	1																			
2	Effort vs. Luck	-0.0852*	1																		
3	Gender	-0.0222*	0.0396*	1																	
4	Age	-0.0464*	-0.0817*	0.0063	1																
5	Number of Children	-0.0620*	-0.0513*	0.0549*	0.4364*	1															
6	Single	0.0450*	0.0498*	-0.0701*	-0.4470*	-0.5196*	1														
7	Married	-0.0415*	-0.0580*	-0.0469*	0.1855*	0.3673*	-0.6341*	1													
8	Education	0.1448*	-0.0290*	-0.0459*	-0.2209*	-0.2336*	0.1520*	-0.0707*	1												
9	Full-time	0.0628*	-0.0102*	-0.2467*	-0.2665*	-0.1447*	0.0355*	0.0271*	0.1930*	1											
10	Part-time Employee	0.0163*	0.0265*	0.1406*	-0.0808*	-0.0133*	0.0139*	0.0023	0.0706*	-0.2500*	1										
11	Self-Employee	0.0097*	-0.0267*	-0.1202*	-0.0157*	0.0411*	-0.0364*	0.0607*	0.0095	-0.2292*	-0.0790*	1									
12	Unemployed	-0.0383*	0.0555*	-0.0221*	-0.0981*	-0.0524*	0.0961*	-0.0925*	-0.0474*	-0.1970*	-0.0679*	-0.0623*	1								
13	Income	0.1270*	-0.0607*	-0.0708*	-0.1734*	-0.0594*	-0.0420*	0.1942*	0.3699*	0.2778*	0.0303*	0.0394*	-0.1201*	1							
14	Size of Town	0.0255*	0.0089	0.0116*	-0.0437*	-0.0881*	0.0713*	-0.0997*	0.2058*	0.0044	0.0283*	-0.0410*	0.0111*	0.0623*	1						
15	Political Orientation	0.0312*	-0.1262*	-0.0019*	0.0784*	0.0809*	-0.0559*	0.0560*	-0.0399*	-0.0359*	-0.0178*	0.0554*	-0.0371*	0.0355*	-0.0533*	1					
16	Competition	-0.0949*	0.3259*	0.0661*	-0.0173*	-0.0052*	0.0330*	-0.0379*	-0.0704*	-0.0584*	0.0310*	-0.0268*	0.0487*	-0.0863*	0.0126*	-0.1179*	1				
17	Trust	-0.1067*	0.0223*	0.0173*	-0.0033*	0.0163*	-0.0038*	-0.0066*	-0.1723*	-0.0650*	-0.0307*	0.0047	0.0418*	-0.1469*	-0.0228*	0.0203*	0.0169*	1			
18	Catholic	0.0079	-0.0019*	0.0108*	-0.0533*	-0.0672*	0.0853*	-0.0457*	0.1182*	0.0023	0.0148*	0.0079	-0.0043*	0.0181*	0.1151*	-0.0222*	0.0300*	0.0255*	1		
19	Protestant	-0.0116*	0.0506*	0.0247*	0.0411*	0.0145*	-0.001*	0.0272*	-0.0651*	-0.0344*	-0.0393*	-0.0109*	-0.0068*	-0.0186*	-0.0837*	-0.0365*	0.0538*	0.1022*	-0.1402*	1	
20	Muslim	0.1079*	-0.0126*	-0.0089*	0.0484*	-0.0153*	-0.0395*	-0.0468*	0.0568*	0.0705*	0.0370*	-0.0314*	-0.0128*	0.0898*	0.0022	0.0119*	-0.0695*	-0.1555*	-0.0854*	-0.6851*	1

Note: '*' denotes significance at 1% level.

Source: World Values Survey (2009).

Table 4.2. *Autonomy Freedom and Control: Full Sample*

	(a)	(b)
Autonomy Freedom	−0.042***	−0.050***
	(0.003)	(0.006)
Sex		0.050**
		(0.021)
Age		−0.006***
		(0.001)
Marital Status		0.010*
		(0.006)
Education		0.041***
		(0.015)
Number of Children		0.016**
		(0.008)
Size of Town		0.002
		(0.005)
Self-employed		−0.028
		(0.049)
Unemployed		0.101**
		(0.050)
Dummies Country	YES	YES
Dummies Time	YES	YES
Weights	YES	YES
Log-Likelihood	−116,491.96	−26,257.52
Number of Observations	53,268	11,951
Overall Significance	3,080.720	1,008.259
Pseudo R^2	0.015	0.018

Notes: ***, ** and * indicate significance at 10%, 5%, and 1% level, respectively. (…) denotes robust standard errors.
Source: World Values Survey (2009).

individual's life turns out seems to increase when he is male and well-educated regardless the marital status of the respondent. Only singles appear in control, if employed.

In columns (g) and (h) of Table 4.4, we divide the sample of individuals in two different groups according to their political orientation. We note that, in spite of whether respondents are left-wing or right-wing politically oriented, the degree of autonomy freedom always affects the level of control individuals hold over the course of their lives. The impact of the demographic control does not present differences across the political orientation of the two groups of respondents. Being young,

Table 4.3. *Autonomy Freedom and Control: Demographic Partition*

	(c) Male	(d) Female	(e) Single	(f) Married
Autonomy Freedom	−0.062*** (0.008)	−0.040*** (0.009)	−0.052*** (0.012)	−0.043*** (0.008)
Sex			0.006*** (0.002)	0.007*** (0.001)
Age	−0.007*** (0.001)	−0.005*** (0.001)	0.031 (0.045)	0.069** (0.029)
Marital Status	0.016* (0.008)	0.003 (0.008)		
Education	0.062*** (0.021)	−0.015 (0.022)	0.075** (0.033)	0.037* (0.021)
Number of Children	0.026** (0.012)	0.008 (0.011)	0.001 (0.032)	0.009 (0.011)
Size of Town	−0.004 (0.007)	0.006 (0.007)	0.021* (0.011)	−0.005 (0.007)
Self-employed	0.006 (0.057)	−0.095 (0.088)	0.133 (0.105)	−0.052 (0.063)
Unemployed	0.187*** (0.068)	−0.003 (0.074)	0.154* (0.080)	−0.008 (0.081)
Dummies Country	YES	YES	YES	YES
Dummies Time	YES	YES	YES	YES
Weights	YES	YES	YES	YES
Log-Likelihood	−12,814.46	−13,572.00	−5,724.08	−14,695.96
Number of Observations	5,852	6,169	2,603	6,724
Overall Significance	485.566	553.459	259.928	587.924
Pseudo R^2	0.019	0.018	0.020	0.019

Notes: ***, **, and * indicate significance at 10%, 5%, and 1% level, respectively. (…) denotes robust standard errors.
Source: World Values Survey (2009).

single, and well-educated raises the probability for a person being in control of her own life, regardless of the political inclinations of the individuals. However, only for those right-leaning politically oriented

Table 4.4. *Autonomy Freedom and Control: Political Partition*

	(g) Left	(h) Right
Autonomy Freedom	−0.051***	−0.043***
	(0.008)	(0.008)
Sex	0.043	0.069**
	(0.030)	(0.029)
Age	−0.006***	−0.007***
	(0.001)	(0.001)
Marital Status	0.016**	0.011**
	(0.008)	(0.006)
Education	0.042**	0.037*
	(0.021)	(0.021)
Number of Children	0.019	0.009
	(0.012)	(0.011)
Size of Town	−0.003	−0.005
	(0.007)	(0.007)
Self-employed	−0.028	−0.052
	(0.074)	(0.063)
Unemployed	0.075	−0.008
	(0.068)	(0.081)
Dummies Country	YES	YES
Dummies Time	YES	YES
Weights	YES	YES
Log-Likelihood	−13,938.99	−14,695.96
Number of Observations	6,327	6,724
Overall Significance	546.366	587.924
Pseudo R^2	0.017	0.019

Notes: ***, **, and * indicate significance at 10%, 5%, and 1% level, respectively. (…) denotes robust standard errors.
Source: World Values Survey (2009).

individuals does gender make a difference, and males appear to be more in control.

In Table 4.5 we partition the sample of individuals on the basis of their religious creed. The results obtained indicate that autonomy freedom explains control over life outcomes for Catholics and Protestants. This result does not apply for Muslims. As far as the demographic controls are concerned, young individuals are more likely to think that effort and hard work, rather than luck and connections, contribute to

Table 4.5. *Autonomy Freedom and Control: Religious Partition*

	(i) Catholics	(j) Muslims	(k) Protestants
Autonomy Freedom	−0.039***	−0.155	−0.063***
	(0.009)	(0.154)	(0.011)
Sex	0.066**	0.177	0.033
	(0.033)	(0.467)	(0.038)
Age	−0.006***	−0.059	−0.004***
	(0.001)	(0.036)	(0.001)
Marital Status	−0.000	0.020	0.031***
	(0.009)	(0.092)	(0.010)
Education	−0.034	0.425*	0.052**
	(0.025)	(0.253)	(0.026)
Number of Children	0.007	0.167	0.020
	(0.012)	(0.257)	(0.015)
Size of Town	−0.006	−0.188*	0.011
	(0.008)	(0.100)	(0.009)
Self-employed	−0.007	1.151	−0.228***
	(0.078)	(0.795)	(0.081)
Unemployed	0.081	2.020**	0.198
	(0.072)	(0.905)	(0.145)
Dummies Country	YES	YES	YES
Dummies Time	YES	YES	YES
Weights	YES	YES	YES
Log-Likelihood	−10,879.28	−78.31	−7,848.40
Number of Observations	4,892	41	3,654
Overall Significance	281.416	33.622	465.030
Pseudo R^2	0.011	0.117	0.030

Notes: ***, **, and * indicate significance at 10%, 5%, and 1% level, respectively. (…) denotes robust standard errors.
Source: World Values Survey (2009).

delivering a better living for Catholics and Protestants. Higher levels of education increase an individual's control over his life for Muslims and Protestants. Finally, greater control over life outcomes seems to increase if the respondent is self-employed for Protestants and just employed for Muslims.

Finally, in Table 4.6 the sample of individuals under scrutiny in our study is divided along geographic lines according to the country where they live. Once again, no matter whether the respondents reside in OECD transition or non-transition countries, higher levels

Table 4.6. *Autonomy Freedom and Control: Geo-economic Partition*

	(l) OECD – Non-transition	(m) OECD – Transition
Autonomy Freedom	−0.058***	−0.030**
	(0.006)	(0.014)
Sex	0.062***	0.020
	(0.022)	(0.054)
Age	−0.005***	−0.007***
	(0.001)	(0.002)
Marital Status	0.014**	−0.004
	(0.006)	(0.015)
Education	0.037**	0.051
	(0.016)	(0.043)
Number of Children	0.017**	0.006
	(0.008)	(0.029)
Size of Town	0.004	−0.010
	(0.005)	(0.016)
Self-Employed	−0.011	−0.127
	(0.048)	(0.169)
Unemployed	0.044	0.229*
	(0.054)	(0.117)
Dummies Country	YES	YES
Dummies Time	YES	YES
Weights	YES	YES
Log-Likelihood	−22,511.20	−3,615.57
Number of observations	10,345	1,606
Overall significance	1,001.301	26.248
Pseudo R^2	0.022	0.005

Notes: ***, **, and * indicate significance at 10%, 5%, and 1% level, respectively. (…) denotes robust standard errors.
Source: World Values Survey (2009).

of an individual's autonomy freedom are constantly associated with greater control over life outcomes. Again, young individuals display stronger preferences for effort, rather than luck and connection, as a determinant of success. However, persons who are male, single, and well-educated and who have numerous children in OECD countries and are employed in transition economies are more likely to possess greater control over their lives.

The analysis carried out so far gives further support to considering the variable *A173 – Freedom of choice and control* as the empirical counterpart of the theoretical measure of autonomy freedom developed in the Freedom of Choice Literature since autonomous individuals who control their choices through a deliberative process in which they form their preferences are also those who retain control over their life outcomes.

Before concluding, it is worth pointing out that our empirical measure of autonomy freedom differs from other established measures of subjective well-being (Praag and Ferrer-i Carbonell 2004; Frey and Stutzer 2002; and Layard 2005). We calculated the correlation coefficients between autonomy freedom and the measures of happiness and self-satisfaction included in the WVS. The correlation coefficients are 0.24 and 0.40, respectively. Although statistically significant at the 1% level, they show that autonomy freedom assesses a different perception of well-being than happiness or self-satisfaction. Furthermore, the small value of the correlation coefficients emphasizes the distinct conceptual base underpinning the three empirical measures. These two considerations highlight that our measure of autonomy freedom is a metric for a proxy of well-being distinct from happiness or self-satisfaction.

4.5 THE AUTONOMOUS PERSON

In this section we comment on some descriptive statistics that show the distribution of autonomous individuals in OECD countries and carry out some empirical estimations to unveil their demographic characteristics as well as their thinking about politics, economics, religion, and society.

The Data

Our first concern is to evaluate whether cross-country differences exist in the level of autonomy freedom. If they do exist, the second step is to examine whether such differences are stable over time both within and across countries.

Figures 4.1 to 4.3 describe the distribution of autonomy freedom in all the OECD countries under investigation as well as for two different subgroups: Transition and non-transition OECD countries. We note that the average level of autonomy freedom differs in the two

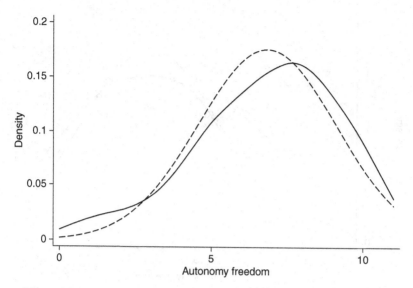

Figure 4.1. Distribution of Autonomy Freedom – All OECD Countries.

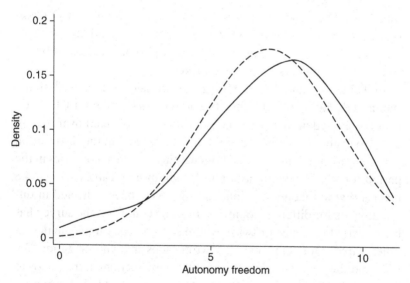

Figure 4.2. Distribution of Autonomy Freedom – OECD Non-transition Countries.

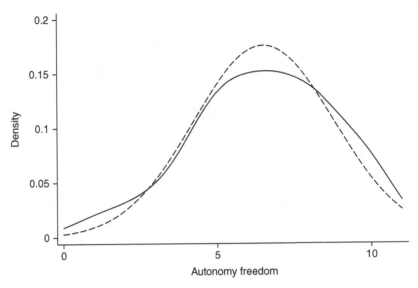

Figure 4.3. Distribution of Autonomy Freedom – OECD Transition Countries.

subgroups of countries: It is higher in non-transition OECD countries and lower in transition OECD economies. Second, the shape of
the distribution does not show significant differences across groups of
countries and appears to be single-picked.

In Tables 4.7 and 4.8 we report the average level as well as the
standard deviation of autonomy freedom in each of the OECD countries considered in this study. The statistics are collected over time in
order to evaluate whether changes in the level and in the distribution
of autonomy freedom occurred both within and across countries in the
period for which data are available. A glimpse at Tables 4.7 and 4.8
reveals that autonomy freedom statistics have been collected in different years for different countries. In some countries, the survey has
been carried out once or twice, whereas it has been implemented in
others three or four times over the two decades under investigation. We
note that the lowest mean value of autonomy freedom corresponds to
Turkey 1996 (4.82) and the highest to Mexico 2000 (8.22). In both cases,
however, the standard deviation is quite high as compared to that of the
other countries (3.31 and 2.22 for Turkey and Mexico, respectively).
This indicates a high dispersion of autonomy freedom values from the
mean which, in turn, implies a great heterogeneity in the population

Table 4.7. *Autonomy Freedom over Time – OECD*

Country	Statistics	1981	1982	1984	1989	1990	1991	1995	1996	1997	1998	1999	2000	2001
Australia	mean sd	7.10 2.11	–	–	–	–	–	7.58 1.97	–	–	–	–	–	–
Austria	mean sd	–	–	–	–	7.59 2.04	–	–	–	–	–	7.47 2.04	–	–
Belgium	mean sd	6.27 2.09	–	–	–	6.55 2.17	–	–	–	–	–	6.56 2.21	–	–
Canada	mean sd	–	7.25 2.10	–	–	7.55 1.80	–	–	–	–	–	–	7.70 1.94	–
Czech Republic	mean sd	–	–	–	–	6.03 2.04	6.84 2.19	–	–	–	6.50 2.02	6.87 2.00	–	–
Denmark	mean sd	7.00 2.13	–	–	–	7.02 1.90	–	–	–	–	–	7.34 1.90	–	–
Finland	mean sd	–	–	–	–	7.65 1.81	–	–	7.67 1.67	–	–	–	7.51 1.75	–
France	mean sd	6.29 2.23	–	–	–	6.24 2.13	–	–	–	–	–	6.46 2.17	–	–
Germany	mean sd	–	–	–	–	6.82 2.08	–	–	–	6.93 2.01	–	7.25 1.83	–	–

(*continued*)

Table 4.7 (*continued*)

Country	Statistics	1981	1982	1984	1989	1990	1991	1995	1996	1997	1998	1999	2000	2001
Greece	mean	–	–	–	–	–	–	–	–	–	–	7.00	–	–
	sd	–	–	–	–	–	–	–	–	–	–	1.83	–	–
Hungary	mean	–	6.83	–	–	–	6.52	–	–	–	6.37	6.20	–	–
	sd	–	2.42	–	–	–	2.44	–	–	–	2.51	2.41	–	–
Iceland	mean	–	–	7.30	–	7.16	–	–	–	–	–	7.60	–	–
	sd	–	–	1.76	–	1.78	–	–	–	–	–	1.48	–	–
Ireland	mean	6.96	–	–	–	7.07	–	–	–	–	–	7.31	–	–
	sd	2.11	–	–	–	2.03	–	–	–	–	–	2.14	–	–
Italy	mean	5.66	–	–	–	6.52	–	–	–	–	–	6.32	–	–
	sd	2.57	–	–	–	2.25	–	–	–	–	–	2.31	–	–
Japan	mean	5.54	–	–	–	5.47	–	5.73	–	–	–	6.00	–	–
	sd	2.13	–	–	–	1.93	–	1.87	–	–	–	1.92	–	–
South Korea	mean	–	5.10	–	–	7.53	–	–	–	–	–	–	–	7.14
	sd	–	2.29	–	–	2.71	–	–	–	–	–	–	–	2.32
Luxembourg	mean	–	–	–	–	–	–	–	–	–	–	6.96	–	–
	sd	–	–	–	–	–	–	–	–	–	–	2.19	–	–

Source: World Values Survey (2009).

Table 4.8. *Autonomy Freedom over Time – OECD*

Country	Statistics	1981	1982	1984	1989	1990	1991	1995	1996	1997	1998	1999	2000	2001
Mexico	mean	–	–	–	–	7.26	–	–	7.48	–	–	–	8.22	–
	sd	–	–	–	–	2.23	–	–	2.20	–	–	–	2.22	–
Netherlands	mean	5.92	–	–	–	6.18	–	–	–	–	–	6.72	–	–
	sd	2.16	–	–	–	2.08	–	–	–	–	–	1.72	–	–
New Zealand	mean	–	–	–	–	–	–	–	–	–	7.84	–	–	–
	sd	–	–	–	–	–	–	–	–	–	1.98	–	–	–
Norway	mean	–	6.64	–	–	7.17	–	–	7.18	–	–	–	–	–
	sd	–	2.28	–	–	2.02	–	–	1.94	–	–	–	–	–
Poland	mean	–	–	–	6.40	6.05	–	–	–	–	–	6.14	–	–
	sd	–	–	–	2.36	2.25	–	–	–	–	–	2.38	–	–
Portugal	mean	–	–	–	–	6.53	–	–	–	–	–	6.88	–	–
	sd	–	–	–	–	2.13	–	–	–	–	–	1.92	–	–
Slovakia	mean	–	–	–	–	5.99	6.93	–	–	–	6.38	6.28	–	–
	sd	–	–	–	–	2.13	2.44	–	–	–	2.10	2.26	–	–

(*continued*)

Table 4.8 (*continued*)

Country	Statistics	1981	1982	1984	1989	1990	1991	1995	1996	1997	1998	1999	2000	2001
Spain	mean	6.49	–	–	–	6.76	–	6.33	–	–	–	6.84	6.72	–
	sd	2.14	–	–	–	1.99	–	2.12	–	–	–	1.93	1.94	–
Sweden	mean	–	7.00	–	–	7.48	–	–	7.26	–	–	7.42	–	–
	sd	–	2.01	–	–	1.85	–	–	1.79	–	–	1.84	–	–
Switzerland	mean	–	–	–	7.36	–	–	–	7.18	–	–	–	–	–
	sd	–	–	–	2.11	–	–	–	2.02	–	–	–	–	–
Turkey	mean	–	–	–	–	–	–	–	4.82	–	–	–	–	5.49
	sd	–	–	–	–	–	–	–	3.31	–	–	–	–	3.37
UK	mean	6.78	–	–	–	7.00	–	–	–	–	–	7.14	–	–
	sd	2.25	–	–	–	2.08	–	–	–	–	–	1.95	–	–
USA	mean	–	7.44	–	–	7.57	–	7.54	–	–	–	7.98	–	–
	sd	–	2.13	–	–	1.91	–	2.02	–	–	–	1.82	–	–

Source: World Values Survey (2009).

in terms of levels of autonomy freedom enjoyed by single individuals. It is also interesting to notice that both mean and standard deviation vary over time. However, while mean values tend to increase as time goes by, standard deviation values do not follow a systematic increasing or decreasing path. This suggests that although autonomy freedom levels seem to have generally gone up over the years under scrutiny, the dispersion of autonomy freedom in OECD countries seems to be quite volatile over time.

In Table 4.9 we show the percentage of low, medium, and high autonomous individuals in the OECD countries under consideration in this study. We note that, to a large extent, the group of individuals who enjoy medium levels of autonomy freedom is the biggest in size. The only exceptions are Turkey, where low autonomous individuals amount to 62.8 pecent of our sample, and South Korea, where 48.7 percent of the individuals interviewed have high autonomy freedom.

In Table 4.10 we divide the individuals in two groups according to their political inclination. We display the distribution of individuals by their level of autonomy freedom and country within each one of these two political groups. We note that there are no significant differences in the distribution of autonomous people across different politically oriented individuals. Across the OECD countries listed in Table 4.9, the largest group of individuals generally enjoys a medium level of autonomy freedom regardless of the political orientation of its members. However, whereas exceptions are more pronounced among individuals with low levels of autonomy freedom in the left politically oriented group, they are more significant among high level of autonomy freedom individuals in the right politically oriented group. More specifically, the exceptions for those left politically oriented are Hungary, Turkey, and France, which respectively display 41, 40.4, 39.5 percent of low autonomy freedom individuals, and South Korea with 58.1 percent of high autonomy freedom individuals. On the other hand, for those individuals who are right politically oriented, the exceptions are Turkey with 54.8 percent of low autonomy freedom individuals and United Kingdom, Mexico, South Korea, New Zealand and Poland which respectively display 55.2, 46.3, 46, 45 and 43.3 percent of high autonomy freedom individuals.

Table 4.9. *Percentage of Autonomous Individuals over the Population*

	Low AF	Medium AF	High AF
Australia	15.6	50.0	34.4
Austria	17.0	47.9	35.1
Belgium	31.5	51.3	17.2
Canada	14.9	54.8	30.3
Czech Republic	32.7	49.5	17.9
Denmark	2.1	59.6	19.0
Finland	11.2	56.4	32.4
France	42.6	42.3	15.1
Germany	2.7	52.6	20.6
Hungary	37.8	38.9	23.2
Iceland	19.9	60.9	19.2
Ireland	19.8	56.5	23.6
Italy	3.1	51.0	18.3
Japan	43.4	52.1	4.5
Republic of Korea	22.7	28.6	48.7
Mexico	20.3	43.6	36.1
Netherlands	31.7	60.4	7.9
New Zealand	12.5	47.6	39.9
Norway	20.8	56.4	22.8
Poland	3.9	45.8	15.5
Portugal	33.7	48.7	17.7
Slovakia	34.3	45.7	20.0
Spain	29.9	50.7	19.4
Sweden	16.2	59.1	24.6
Switzerland	20.2	52.9	26.9
Turkey	62.8	17.8	19.4
UK	23.2	54.6	22.2

Source: World Values Survey (2009).

Finally, in Table 4.11 we show the distribution of individuals by their level of autonomy freedom in each one of the OECD countries and according to their respective religious beliefs. Again, the largest group of individuals generally displays medium levels of autonomy freedom, regardless of the religion of its members. However, there are some exceptions. South Korea, Mexico, New Zealand, and United Kingdom are all countries that show percentages over 40 percent of high autonomy freedom individuals no matter of their religious beliefs. The same applies to Turkey, which exhibits high percentages of high autonomy

Table 4.10. *Percentage of Autonomous Individuals over the Population: Political Partition*

	Left Wing			Right Wing		
	Low AF	Medium AF	High AF	Low AF	Medium AF	High AF
Australia	20.1	49.6	30.3	16.6	50.3	33.1
Austria	19.8	46.8	33.4	17.4	46.2	36.5
Belgium	31.3	50.8	17.9	29.4	48.9	21.7
Canada	17.1	51.2	31.7	14.7	51.4	33.9
Czech Republic	36.8	46.9	16.3	26.1	51.4	22.5
Denmark	23.8	53.5	22.7	19.4	53.5	27.2
Finland	13.4	57.0	29.6	11.0	56.4	32.6
France	39.5	44.3	16.2	33.9	46.0	20.1
Germany	26.7	52.9	20.4	19.9	54.7	25.4
Greece	23.4	57.1	19.5	18.1	58.3	23.5
Hungary	41.0	38.4	20.6	32.9	39.7	27.4
Iceland	19.2	60.3	20.5	12.4	61.6	26.0
Ireland	24.9	51.1	24.1	18.7	51.9	29.4
Italy	36.6	46.5	16.9	34.5	43.1	22.4
Japan	35.5	53.4	11.1	37.8	46.1	16.0
South Korea	18.6	23.3	58.1	25.9	28.1	46.0
Luxembourg	24.5	49.7	25.8	24.1	48.9	27.0
Mexico	18.3	41.9	39.8	17.4	36.3	46.3
Netherlands	26.9	64.4	8.8	33.2	55.9	10.9
New Zealand	18.2	42.6	39.1	9.8	45.2	45.0
Norway	27.8	51.7	20.6	20.5	52.7	26.8
Poland	30.2	31.4	38.4	27.0	29.7	43.3
Portugal	29.7	50.5	19.9	27.7	51.7	20.6
Slovakia	37.8	44.7	17.6	32.0	43.3	24.7
Spain	29.9	50.1	20.0	26.5	48.1	25.4
Sweden	21.4	56.0	22.6	14.9	55.8	29.3
Switzerland	23.9	50.8	25.3	19.0	46.7	34.3
Turkey	40.4	19.4	40.2	54.8	16.4	28.9
United Kingdom	25.8	53.0	21.2	13.6	31.2	55.2
United States	18.3	47.1	34.6	15.0	46.8	38.2

Source: World Values Survey (2009).

Table 4.11. *Percentage of Autonomous Individuals over the Population: Religious Partition*

	Catholics			Muslim			Orhtodox			Protestant		
	Low Af	Midium AF	High AF	Low Af	Midium AF	High AF	Low Af	Midium AF	High AF	Low Af	Midium AF	High AF
Australia	19.3	49.6	31.1	18.5	51.9	29.6	17.6	52.3	30.1	16.5	51.1	32.4
Austria	18.5	46.4	35.1	18.0	44.5	37.5	18.4	44.2	37.4	17.6	45.8	36.6
Belgium	29.8	50.1	20.1	30.5	48.3	21.2	30.0	49.0	21.0	30.7	48.3	21.0
Canada	16.1	50.7	33.2	17.0	51.1	31.8	17.0	51.0	32.0	15.9	51.9	32.2
Czech Republic	30.3	49.8	19.9	27.9	52.5	19.6	27.9	52.5	19.6	28.6	52.0	19.3
Denmark	21.1	48.5	30.4	19.5	50.5	30.0	19.0	51.1	29.9	21.2	54.0	24.8
Finland	12.1	52.8	35.1	10.6	52.0	37.4	10.5	53.3	36.3	11.6	58.3	30.1
France	37.5	44.9	17.6	39.0	44.7	16.3	38.6	44.8	16.6	38.4	45.0	16.5
Germany	25.4	52.9	21.7	28.4	51.4	20.2	28.4	51.4	20.2	25.0	52.9	22.1
Greece	16.4	58.2	25.4	16.0	62.0	22.0	21.0	58.0	20.9	16.0	62.0	22.0
Hungary	36.4	39.1	24.5	35.1	41.5	23.4	35.4	41.6	23.0	34.6	40.4	25.0
Iceland	14.5	55.4	30.1	12.5	58.3	29.2	12.5	58.3	29.2	15.5	61.4	23.1
Ireland	21.0	51.7	27.3	22.9	51.9	25.2	22.7	52.3	25.0	22.2	52.4	25.4
Italy	35.5	44.8	19.7	31.1	47.2	21.7	31.0	47.3	21.7	31.4	47.2	21.4
Japan	36.8	48.6	14.6	36.9	48.6	14.5	36.4	48.6	15.0	36.8	48.6	14.6
South Korea	23.3	26.3	50.4	24.3	26.0	49.7	24.4	25.9	49.7	22.6	26.7	50.7
Luxembourg	24.0	49.1	26.9	26.5	47.7	25.8	25.9	48.5	25.6	26.1	48.3	25.6

Mexico	17.6	38.2	44.1	17.6	36.8	45.6	17.7	37.1	45.2	18.5	37.8	43.7
Netherlands	26.1	63.8	10.1	22.5	66.4	11.1	22.5	66.6	10.9	27.0	62.7	10.3
New Zealand	13.5	44.1	42.4	13.7	45.5	40.8	14.0	45.9	40.2	12.6	44.9	42.5
Norway	23.0	51.3	25.7	21.7	52.8	25.5	21.0	52.4	26.6	24.0	52.6	23.4
Poland	28.5	30.6	40.9	32.8	42.3	24.8	32.7	41.9	25.5	32.2	41.7	26.0
Portugal	28.7	51.2	20.1	22.1	54.2	23.7	22.1	54.2	23.7	22.5	53.6	23.9
Slovakia	34.9	43.6	21.5	30.4	46.9	22.7	30.5	46.5	22.9	31.5	47.5	21.1
Spain	28.3	49.2	22.5	30.8	47.6	21.6	30.8	47.4	21.8	30.7	47.6	21.7
Sweden	19.6	55.1	25.2	19.4	55.0	25.5	18.8	55.3	25.9	18.5	54.8	26.6
Switzerland	21.4	47.6	31.0	23.2	46.4	30.4	22.9	45.5	31.6	20.8	49.3	29.9
Turkey	19.3	6.4	74.3	47.3	18.0	34.7	19.2	6.4	74.4	19.2	6.3	74.6
United Kingdom	12.8	28.0	59.3	11.0	23.5	65.5	11.0	23.1	65.9	17.7	37.5	44.8
United States	16.4	48.4	35.2	15.9	48.2	36.0	15.4	48.6	36.0	16.5	46.6	36.9

Source: World Values Survey (2009).

freedom individuals among Catholics, Orthodoxes, and Protestants. Turkey, however, shows also a relevant percentage of low autonomous individuals (47.3 percent) among its Muslim population.

The Empirical Methodology

Our next step is to examine who are the autonomous individuals and what they think about politics, economics, religion, and society. With this purpose in mind, we estimate the following ordered logistic model:

$$AF^s_{i,c,t} = \alpha Dmg^s_{i,c,t} + \beta Pol^s_{i,c,t} + \gamma Soc^s_{i,c,t} + \delta Econ^s_{i,c,t} + \theta Rlig^s_{i,c,t} + \varepsilon^s_{i,c,t}$$
$$(4.2)$$

where $AF^s_{i,c,t}$ measures the level of autonomy freedom of individual i in country c at time t. *Dmg* is a vector of demographic characteristics of respondents including sex, age, marital status, education level, income, and employment status; *Pol* reflects the individual's political orientation; *Soc* measures the individual's level of trust in other people; *Econ* indicates the individual's support for market-oriented institutions; *Rlig* is a vector reflecting the religious beliefs of the respondents, and ε is the i.i.d. error term.

The superscript s in the equation indicates that in carrying out the empirical analysis we consider the full sample (in which case s = full sample) as well as different subsamples divided along geo-economic lines (s = individuals living either in OECD transition or OECD non-transition countries), and on the basis of the political orientation of the respondents (s = either left-wing or right-wing party supporters) and their religious beliefs (s = either Catholics, Muslims, or Protestants).

Before moving to the estimation, it is important to stress that the empirical results that we obtain do not allow us to establish any causal relationship between the two sides of equation 4.2, but only conditional correlations. We believe that such correlations are interesting since, beside being statistically robust, they allow us to establish some characteristics that identify autonomous individuals, in general and across countries, as well as his political orientation and religious beliefs.

Finally, note that these empirical results cannot be interpreted in prescriptive terms. The traits of the autonomous individuals that emerge from our investigation ought to be considered as a snapshot taken in a specific moment in time. This implies that policy interventions supporting autonomy freedom may change over time as the identikit of the autonomous person changes, both within and across countries.

Estimation Results

In Table 4.12 we report regression results for the full sample. In column (a) we find that the probability of high levels of autonomy freedom increases for those individuals with the following demographic characteristics: male, either young or old, rather than middle-aged, with no or a low number of children, married, well-educated, employed (especially self-employed), rich, and living in big cities. It is interesting to note that the interaction between education and income has a positive and significant effect on the probability of being autonomous. This indicates that the positive and significant effect of education on an individual's probability of being autonomous is strengthened by an increase in the level of her income.

In column (b) we assess what autonomous individuals think about politics, economics, and society. We find that they are more likely to be right-wing politically oriented, free market supporters, and inclined to trust other people. It is important to note that both the signs and coefficients of demographic variables are consistent across the two specifications displayed in columns (a) and (b). The only exception are the marital status and the size of town of the respondents that are no longer significant, although the estimates show the same sign.

In column (c) we add the individuals' religious beliefs. Again, the demographic characteristics of autonomous individuals and their opinions about politics, economics, and society are unaffected. As far as their religious beliefs are concerned, we note that the likelihood of being autonomous is not affected by the religious faith of the respondents.

In Table 4.13 we divide the full sample along geo-economic lines according to whether individuals live in OECD transition (column (d), (e) and (f)) and OECD non-transition (columns (g), (h) and (i)). Though results do not change much across specifications, a more careful look at the estimates reveals some differences across the two subsamples, which deserves to be noted. The probability of being

Table 4.12. *Autonomous Individuals: Who Are They? – Full Sample*

	(a)	(b)	(c)
Gender	−0.031**	−0.023*	−0.021
	(−2.50)	(−1.66)	(−1.35)
Age	−0.016***	−0.018***	−0.019***
	(−6.36)	(−6.28)	(−5.92)
Age^2	0.000***	0.000***	0.000***
	(6.08)	(5.82)	(5.64)
Number of Children	−0.023***	−0.023***	−0.019***
	(−4.26)	(−3.87)	(−2.87)
Single	−0.034*	−0.025	−0.035
	(−1.79)	(−1.18)	(−1.44)
Education	0.070***	0.055***	0.058***
	(7.95)	(5.58)	(5.13)
Full-time Employee	0.006	−0.005	−0.007
	(0.35)	(−0.27)	(−0.32)
Part-time Employee	−0.016	−0.014	−0.01
	(−0.71)	(−0.56)	(−0.36)
Self-Employee	0.089***	0.055*	0.054
	(3.12)	(1.76)	(1.48)
Unemployed	−0.107***	−0.107***	−0.078*
	(−3.40)	(−3.00)	(−1.87)
Income	0.035***	0.031***	0.033***
	(13.02)	(10.40)	(9.76)
Size of Town	0.005*	0.005	0.005
	(1.70)	(1.59)	(1.57)
Political Orientation		0.020***	0.016***
		(5.52)	(3.74)
Competition		−0.032***	−0.033***
		(−9.76)	(−8.67)
Trust		−0.108***	−0.110***
		(−7.59)	(−6.90)
Catholic			−0.004
			(−0.12)
Protestant			0.018
			(0.50)
Muslim			−0.203
			(−1.63)
Year Dummies	YES	YES	YES
Country Dummies	YES	YES	YES
Weights	YES	YES	YES
Number of observations	35565	29049	21700
Log-Likelihood	−71700	−57900	−43300
Overall Significance	2686.501	2331.812	1934.707
Pseudo R^2	0.023	0.024	0.026

Notes: ***, **, and * indicate significance at 10%, 5%, and 1% level, respectively. (...) denotes robust standard errors.
Source: World Values Survey (2009).

Table 4.13. *Autonomous Individuals: Who Are They? – Geo-economic Partition*

	OECD Transition Economies			OECD Non-transition Economies		
	(d)	(e)	(f)	(g)	(h)	(i)
Gender	−0.087***	−0.045	−0.011	−0.018	−0.017	−0.023
	(−2.85)	(−1.34)	(−0.28)	(−1.30)	(−1.13)	(−1.36)
Age	−0.007	−0.017**	−0.021**	−0.017***	−0.017***	−0.018***
	(−1.07)	(−2.20)	(−2.21)	(−6.33)	(−5.60)	(−5.33)
Age^2	0.000	0.000*	0.000**	0.000***	0.000***	0.000***
	(0.31)	(1.80)	(1.99)	(6.49)	(5.37)	(5.15)
Number of Children	−0.011	−0.000	0.017	−0.025***	−0.026***	−0.023***
	(−0.69)	(−0.01)	(0.81)	(−4.48)	(−4.15)	(−3.26)
Single	−0.005	0.066	0.073	−0.040**	−0.040*	−0.050*
	(−0.08)	(1.01)	(0.93)	(−1.97)	(−1.77)	(−1.93)
Education	0.105***	0.071***	0.048	0.067***	0.054***	0.060***
	(4.47)	(2.78)	(1.47)	(7.03)	(5.08)	(5.00)
Full-time Employee	−0.072*	−0.041	−0.028	0.02	0.006	−0.003
	(−1.66)	(−0.85)	(−0.47)	−1.12	−0.3	(−0.14)
Part-time Employee	−0.083	−0.104	−0.08	−0.008	−0.005	−0.005
	(−0.92)	(−1.06)	(−0.74)	(−0.33)	(−0.20)	(−0.18)
Self-Employee	0.188**	0.225**	0.266**	0.073**	0.034	0.031
	(2.21)	(2.33)	(1.98)	(2.43)	(1.03)	(0.83)
Unemployed	−0.128*	−0.106	−0.11	−0.112***	−0.114***	−0.075
	(−1.82)	(−1.36)	(−1.29)	(−3.21)	(−2.85)	(−1.56)
Income	0.051***	0.044***	0.057***	0.031***	0.028***	0.030***
	(6.95)	(5.57)	(5.62)	(10.92)	(8.61)	(8.15)
Size of Town	0.01	0.001	0.009	0.003	0.006	0.005
	(1.48)	(0.18)	(1.01)	(1.06)	(1.64)	(1.32)

(continued)

Table 4.13 (*continued*)

	OECD Transition Economies			OECD Non-transition Economies		
	(d)	(e)	(f)	(g)	(h)	(i)
Political Orientation		0.038***	0.033***		0.015***	0.012***
		(4.59)	(3.26)		(3.72)	(2.58)
Competition		−0.033***	−0.036***		−0.032***	−0.032***
		(−4.15)	(−3.68)		(−8.88)	(−7.92)
Trust		−0.100***	−0.077		−0.108***	−0.113***
		(−2.58)	(−1.59)		(−7.06)	(−6.68)
Muslim			−0.187			−0.199
			(−1.53)			(−1.61)
Catholic			−0.045			0.002
			(−0.40)			(0.04)
Protestant			0.005			0.019
			(0.04)			(0.50)
Year Dummies	YES	YES	YES	YES	YES	YES
Country Dummies	YES	YES	YES	YES	YES	YES
Weights	YES	YES	YES	YES	YES	YES
Number of observations	5703	4752	3061	29862	24297	18639
Log-Likelihood	−12000	−9803.09	−6368.28	−59500	−48000	−36900
Overall Significance	266.385	230.049	128.9	2027.114	1810.138	1470.086
Pseudo R^2	0.013	0.014	0.012	0.021	0.022	0.023

Notes: ***, **, and * indicate significance at 10% , 5%, and 1% level, respectively. (...) denotes robust standard errors.
Source: World Values Survey (2009).

autonomous increases for those individuals displaying the following demographic characteristics: either young or old, well-educated, rich, right-wing politically oriented, market supporters, and inclined to trust other people. Being self-employed is significantly correlated with autonomy freedom for respondents living in OECD transition countries. In OECD non-transition economies, however, the probability of being autonomous increases if individuals have no (or a low number of) children.

In Table 4.14 we divide the full sample into two smaller subsamples according to political orientation. Our findings are displayed in columns (j) and (k). Regardless of the sample of individuals under consideration (right-wing or left-wing supporters), autonomous individuals are more likely to be either young or old, with no or a low number of children, well-educated, rich, market supporters, and inclined to trust other people. However, right-wing politically oriented individuals are more likely to be autonomous if they are married, self-employed, and live in big cities. On the other hand, the probability of being autonomous increases for left-wing politically oriented only if they are employed. As far as the religious beliefs of respondents are concerned, autonomous individuals are less likely to be Protestants for right-wing party supporters and Muslims for left-wing party supporters.

Finally, in Table 4.15 the full sample is divided in three different subsamples according to religious beliefs. This generates three different specifications whose estimates are reported in columns (l) to (n). The results differ widely across estimations. As far as Catholics are concerned (column (l)), we note that autonomous individuals are either young or old, well-educated, employed, and rich. Autonomous Catholics also show right-wing political attitudes, support market competition, and trust other people.

In column (m) the results indicate that Muslims are likely to be more autonomous if they are male, married, with no or a low number of children, wage-employed, and rich and live in big cities. It is interesting to note that age does not seem to affect the probability of being autonomous for Muslims. This is due to the fact that the relationship is not quadratic. Therefore, we reestimated the specification in column (m) assuming linearity in age. The results, which are not displayed in the table, show that Muslim autonomous individuals are

Table 4.14. *Autonomous Individuals: Who Are They? –*
Political Partition

	Left	Right
	(j)	**(k)**
Gender	−0.032	0.007
	(−1.49)	(0.35)
Age	−0.018***	−0.016***
	(−4.11)	(−4.04)
Age^2	0.000***	0.000***
	(3.90)	(3.95)
Number of Children	−0.017*	−0.022***
	(−1.86)	(−2.60)
Single	−0.008	−0.072**
	(−0.23)	(−2.21)
Education	0.060***	0.049***
	−3.97	−3.26
Full-time Employee	(0.004)	(−0.007)
	(−0.15)	−0.26
Part-time Employee	0.023	−0.057
	(0.62)	(−1.50)
Self-Employed	0.064	0.095**
	(1.22)	(2.11)
Unemployed	−0.150***	−0.014
	(−2.79)	(−0.27)
Income	0.038***	0.032***
	(8.11)	(7.10)
Size of Town	0.001	0.012**
	(0.25)	(2.52)
Competition	−0.026***	−0.040***
	(−5.12)	(−8.16)
Trust	−0.123***	−0.075***
	(−5.66)	(−3.57)
Catholic	−0.007	−0.068
	(−0.15)	(−1.51)
Protestant	0.046	−0.085*
	(0.93)	(−1.84)
Muslim	−0.277**	−0.049
	(−1.99)	(−0.29)
Year Dummies	YES	YES
Country Dummies	YES	YES
Weights	YES	YES
Number of Observations	12008	12721
Log-Likelihood	−24100	−25400
Overall Significance	1037.686	1256.048
Pseudo R^2	0.023	0.032

Notes: ***, **, and * indicate significance at 10%, 5%, and 1% level,
respectively. (...) denotes robust standard errors.
Source: World Values Survey (2009).

Table 4.15. *Autonomous Individuals: Who Are They? – Religious Partition*

	Catholic	**Muslim**	**Protestant**
	(l)	**(m)**	**(n)**
Sex	−0.010	−0.361***	0.027
	(0.022)	(0.086)	(0.028)
Age	−0.015***	−0.001	−0.033***
	(0.004)	(0.019)	(0.006)
Age^2	0.000***	0.000	0.000***
	(0.000)	(0.000)	(0.000)
Number of Children	−0.008	−0.088***	−0.020
	(0.009)	(0.027)	(0.012)
Single	0.051	−0.398***	−0.094**
	(0.035)	(0.117)	(0.042)
Education	0.052***	0.086	0.067***
	(0.016)	(0.061)	(0.019)
Full-time Employed	−0.039	−0.119	0.017
	(0.029)	(0.103)	(0.040)
Part-time Employee	−0.012	−0.141	−0.047
	(0.040)	(0.154)	(0.052)
Self-Employed	0.058	−0.255**	0.125**
	(0.050)	(0.123)	(0.062)
Unemployed	−0.107**	0.008	−0.208**
	(0.052)	(0.129)	(0.086)
Income	0.033***	0.070***	0.040***
	(0.005)	(0.023)	(0.006)
Size of Town	−0.005	0.031**	0.006
	(0.005)	(0.015)	(0.006)
Competition	−0.028***	−0.020	−0.042***
	(0.005)	(0.013)	(0.008)
Political Orientation	0.026***	−0.069***	0.024***
	(0.006)	(0.016)	(0.008)
Trust	−0.103***	0.255**	−0.129***
	(0.022)	(0.124)	(0.028)
Year Dummies	YES	YES	YES
Country Dummies	YES	YES	YES
Weights	YES	YES	YES
Number of Observations	−23,454.21	−2,075.83	−13,034.89
Log-Likelihood	11,660	1,022	6,937
Overall Significance	1,112.593	554.052	5,053.519
Pseudo R^2	0.028	0.032	0.022

Notes: ***, **, and * indicate significance at 10%, 5%, and 1% level, respectively. (...) denotes robust standard errors.
Source: World Values Survey (2009).

more likely to be young. The political orientation of the respondents plays a role for Muslims: left-wing party supporters are more likely to be autonomous. Finally, autonomous Muslims are less likely to trust other people in society.

Estimates in column (n) indicate that Protestants are more likely to be autonomous if young or old, married, well-educated, employed – and more so if self-employed – rich, right-wing politically oriented, confident in market competition, and trusting other people.

4.6 WRAPPING UP OUR RESULTS

Despite the efforts displayed in the last three decades or so to develop measures of freedom of choice at the theoretical level, no explicit attempt has yet been made to provide an empirical counterpart for these measures. In this chapter we argued that a particular question posed by the WVS *A173 – How much freedom of choice and control* fills the gap and, at the same time, can be based upon sound theoretical foundations, namely, the autonomy freedom ranking based on the Millian concept of individuality.

Our claim has been established by means of an analytic study of the correspondence between the WVS question and the conceptual underpinnings of the theoretical measure of autonomy freedom. Such an interpretation of freedom is then translated in this chapter into an empirical measure and the empirical measure, in turn, is operationalized by collecting individual level data across OECD countries over a time span covering the period 1981–2004 and by examining who the autonomous individuals are and what they think about economics, politics, religion, and society.

Though our exercise entails no more than (statistically robust) correlations and does not allow to extract causal or prescriptive conclusions, autonomous individuals, by and large, display the following demographic characteristics: male, either young or old, with no or a low number of children, single, well-educated, employed, rich, and living in big cities. These people are also more likely to be right-wing party supporters, free market oriented, and more inclined to trust others.

Beside its contribution to the quantitative assessment of autonomy freedom, our empirical measure may be useful to scholars interested in the analysis of the relationship between autonomy freedom and the functioning of democracy and the economy. The measure, in particular, may contribute to answering questions concerning the mechanisms of economic policy design as well as the process of collective decision making that are still unanswered. Here are some examples.

A vast literature stresses the significance of human capital as a source of competitive advantage to individuals, organizations, and societies. Individuals' perception of autonomy freedom – their perception of being conscious subjects, masters of their own destinies – is likely to be correlated with the production of human capital and, in turn, with economic innovation and growth. Undertaking tasks whose design emerges from an autonomous deliberative process strengthens individuals' responsibilities and expands the return of investment in human capital. We believe that this value-generating potential of freedom may lead to formulate interesting questions that deserve to be investigated: Does the degree of autonomy freedom affect the process of innovation and technological change? Does it influence entrepreneurial activities? Does it impact on social mobility? What are the implications that can be derived from answering these questions for economic growth, the distribution of income, and human well-being?

Individuals' perception of autonomy freedom is also likely to be connected with how democracy works. It has been argued that the performance of democratic systems (as well as their consolidation) depends on civic virtues (i.e., a well-functioning social organization based on networks, norms, and social trust that facilitates coordination, cooperation, and independent civic engagement). Other scholars pointed out that the working of democracies is crucially dependent on a widespread sense of autonomy in political choices. As civic virtues and autonomy flourish, so does political accountability and therefore the responsiveness of collective decision making to the individual preferences held in a society. In this framework, it is possible to identify a relationship between the perception of autonomy freedom in political choices in a virtuous society and the political responsibility in the process of democratic decision making. Interesting research questions worth exploring are: Do higher levels of autonomy freedom bear consequences on representativeness in elected assemblies? Do they affect policy decisions at different governmental levels? What is the effect of greater autonomy freedom on electoral campaigning and on parties' electoral strategies? Do variations in the degree of autonomy freedom affect political accountability of elected representatives?

PART II

AUTONOMY FREEDOM AND THE
WELFARE STATE

5

Why Redistribute?

5.1 INTRODUCTION

Drawing from classical political economy, the framers of the U.S. constitution argued in favor of extending the suffrage only to citizens who were property owners. They believed that universal enfranchisement would have likely overturned the right to property.

In modern democracies political rights are distributed equally and actual income distributions are such that the median income is generally lower than the average income. Under these circumstances a majority of voters (i.e., the poorer 50 percent) may likely be expected to impose a transfer scheme that redistributes all income to the mean. However, history offers no evidence in support of this expectation: Universal suffrage did not lead to the expropriation of the wealthy by the poor. How is this possible? Why does inequality persist in democracies? Why does the majority of citizens with incomes below the median not form a cohesive block of voters to approve extensive welfare systems? To answer these questions we review the literature that explains the *redistribution paradox* in democratic systems. This line of research, though vast and articulated, shares the common view that income differences are, to a significant extent, an outcome of the political process.

We also know that income inequality is justifiable in democracies and that the poor majority does not expropriate the wealthy minority properties. However, governments of all hues design redistributive schemes to limit income differences. Such redistributive policies vary across countries. Why does this happen? Why do some countries spend more on welfare and others less? Do individual preferences for redistribution help explain differences in welfare spending across countries? To answer these and related questions, we review the literature on the determinants of people's preferences for redistribution and their effects on the extent of welfare spending. More specifically, we examine the effects of people's beliefs about social mobility on the distribution of income, analyze the consequences of concern for fairness on individual's attitudes toward inequality and describe further economic, social, political, and cultural motivations that explain the cross-country heterogeneity in social expenditure.

5.2 THE REDISTRIBUTION PARADOX

Why in democracies does the poor majority not expropriate the wealth of the rich through large-scale income redistributions? For decades this research question featured prominently amongst scholars in the fields of political economy and political science. Various arguments have been put forward to shed light on this apparently puzzling phenomenon.[1]

One explanation why income equalization is not carried out through political action in democracies refers to the view that large-scale wealth expropriation would produce adverse dynamic effects for the entire economy. In the tradition of classical economists, a significant redistribution of income from more to less productive economic agents is opposed as inefficient. Redistributive policies would cause an overall reduction of working incentives and a decline of national income with the consequence that the wealth of the majority would inevitably fall (Meltzer and Richards, 1981). Further, if the rich have an exit option by moving to another jurisdiction, this would tend to limit the available resources and ultimately the scope for redistribution (Epple and Romer, 1991).

In the same vein, other scholars argue that more egalitarian distributions of income are unlikely to be associated with investments in education, innovation, and economic growth (Perotti, 1993; Fernandez and

---

[1] For an interesting analysis of the political economy of unequal income distribution in democratic countries, see Putterman, Roemer, and Sylvestre (1998) and Harms and Zink (2003). For extensive overviews on the political economy of social security, see Persson and Tabellini (2000) and Galasso and Profeta (2002).

Rogerson, 1995). Benhabib and Rustichini (1991) point out that incentives to invest in human capital and productive knowledge conducive to higher growth are positively correlated with income inequality. Similarly, Saint Paul and Verdier (1996) claim that more inequality may pave the way to higher growth when the economy experiences government spending in the form of public education.[2] In this framework, voters understand these unfavorable effects of income equality on economic development and rationally choose to attenuate their requests for higher wealth redistribution.

A second strand of arguments to explain why in capitalist democracies extensive reduction of income inequality are not implemented through the electoral process questions the assumption that democracy expresses the will of the people. This view is connected with the ideas developed by the Virginia School of Public Choice (Buchanan and Tullock, 1962). Within this line of research, Olson (1965) suggests that, due to the free rider problem, small groups are better equipped in swaying policy choices than large (and often disorganized) groups. Since democratic policy makers are captured by the will of organized pressure groups, the interests of less influential groups are less effectively supported (Kristov, Lindert, and McClelland, 1992; Coate and Morris, 1995). Moreover, small and more organized groups can offer larger per-capita gains and, thus, mobilize more effectively their members by providing stronger incentives (Peltzman, 1976).

In modern democracies the distribution of political influence in favor of small and organized groups is generally associated to their better economic conditions. Breyer and Ursprung (1998) demonstrate that economic power often translates into political power. They argue that in representative democracies in which politicians and parties need considerable financial support to fund their electoral campaigns, there are significant opportunities for the rich to resist the introduction of confiscatory taxation that moderates income inequality. Furthermore, since the various groups that participate in the political process face different political and economic costs of obtaining transfers, policy makers are more likely to enact programs that redistribute

---

[2] Theory and empirical evidence on the relationship between redistribution and economic growth are not univocal. Opinions supporting the view that inequality is harmful for growth are expressed by Persson and Tabellini (1992, 1994), Alesina and Rodrik (1994), and Birdsall, Ross, and Sabot (1995).

wealth across groups with similar incomes, rather than aiming at large-scale equalization (Dougan and Snyder, 1993; Mueller and Stratmann, 2003).

Another important explanation for the nonexpropriation of income in democratic systems is connected with the concept of *voters ignorance*. Voters ignorance is rational since the cost of acquiring information about the legislative process is, for the vast majority of voters, higher than the expected benefits (Olson, 1965; Popkin, 1991; Bartels, 1996), while, at the same time, the effect of this acquisition on their welfare is negligible. Rosenstone and Hansen (1993) suggest that poor and less-educated persons have a lower propensity in spending time and money to acquire information about the policy formation process. Furthermore the media, which to a large extent influences the political opinion of voters, is owned or controlled by economically powerful groups that are interested in maintaining a relatively unfettered process of wealth accumulation (Chomsky and Herman, 1988; Zaller, 1992).

The way in which opposing parties face competition may constitute another interesting, possible, explanation why democracy does not allow full redistribution of wealth. Drawing from one of his previous studies, Roemer (1998) highlights that electoral competition is never based on a single issue, but it is characterized by parties confronting themselves on multi-issue platforms among which many have a noneconomic nature.[3] He constructs a theoretical model in which voters preferences are defined over wealth and some noneconomic issues. In this context, parties do not maximize the probability of winning per se, but their constituents' expected welfare. He argues that redistribution schemes are not directly put to a vote since they are an element of the parties' policy platforms. If political competition takes place within a context in which a noneconomic issue plays a salient role, the party representing the poor may advocate a softened redistribution policy.[4]

---

[3] See Poole and Rosenthal (1991) for multi-issue political competition in the United States. See also Laver and Hunt (1992) and Kitschelt (1994) for multi-issue political competition in European countries. See also Kalyvas (1996) and Przeworski and Sprague (1986) for political competition fought on the basis of economic (income redistribution) and noneconomic (religion) issues in European politics.

[4] A related literature focuses on political economy models of optimal social policy mixture. Bethencourt Marrero and Galasso (2001) consider health care and social security; Boldrin and Montes (2005) investigate the joint determination of public education and

Social limits to redistribution might arise also when economic inequality has an informational value for signaling people's social status. Borrowing from a related sociological literature (Lipset, 1967), Corneo and Grüner (2000) hypothesize that social recognition plays a crucial role in shaping individuals' policy attitudes. They claim that company of richer persons provides higher social status and argue that the policy position over redistribution of middle-class voters may be affected by their desire for social success.[5] In this context, middle-class voters who derive financial gains from redistribution still do not advocate such a policy because signaling their middle-class social status (i.e., differentiating themselves from their social competitors) becomes more difficult as the distribution of disposable income becomes more equal.

5.3 SOCIAL MOBILITY AND REDISTRIBUTION

The classic argument that describes people's preferences for redistribution is based on the net pecuniary gain obtained by individuals from redistributive taxation. This view states that, if an individual is a direct recipient of a transfer program, she favors it and vice versa (Roberts, 1977; Meltzer and Richards, 1981).

In Figure 5.1 we show a positive relationship between individual preferences for income differences and their self-reported income. The countries under consideration in the figure are all OECD members. Though not very pronounced, the relationship, is positive. This indicates that the higher individual income, the stronger her preferences for income differences and, as a consequence, the lower her support for income transfers. In Figure 5.2 we note a direct relationship between social expenditure as percentage of GDP in the OECD countries and a measure of the individual's net gain from redistributive taxation. More specifically, on the horizontal axis we calculate at the country level the difference between the average self-reported income

pension spending. Boeri, Conde-Ruiz, and Galasso (2003) analyze employment protection legislation and unemployment insurance programs. Conde-Ruiz and Galasso (2003) model retirement timing provisions together with pensions.

[5] Cole, Mailath, and Postlewaite (1992) define this situation as social competition as opposed to market competition. People compete in order to preserve or improve their social environment.

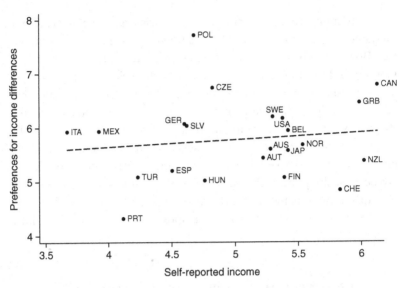

Figure 5.1. Income and Preferences for Income Differences.

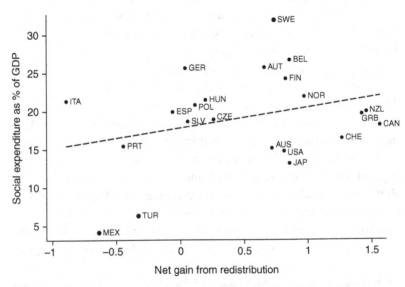

Figure 5.2. Net Gain from Redistribution and Social Expenditure.

in society and an individual's self-reported income. A move from the origin to the right on the horizontal axis indicates a move from countries where, on average, there are more individuals with self-reported income higher than societal self-reported income to countries where, on average, individuals display self-reported income lower than societal self-reported income. Therefore, a move from the left to the right in Figure 5.2 indicates a decrease in the individuals' net loss from redistributive taxation. The relationship is clearly positive indicating that countries with higher individual incomes display lower levels of welfare spending.

However, since taxes and redistributive schemes are in place for lengthy periods, individuals are interested not only in today's income after taxes but also in future incomes. Therefore, people are likely to maximize a multiperiod utility function in which income at further stages will be properly discounted. In this context, people's beliefs about social mobility play a crucial role in shaping their attitudes toward redistribution. Individuals whose income is currently below the average expect that they or their children will someday move up in the income ladder and oppose high taxes, fearing that it would hurt their own or their children's future.

In the horizontal axis of Figure 5.3, we measure people's perception about the working of income mobility by asking them how big are the chances for the poor to work their way out of poverty. The more we move to the right on the horizontal axis of the figure the greater people's perception that incomes are not mobile in the society where they live. The relationship between the individual's beliefs about income mobility and social spending shown in Figure 5.3 indicates that, in the OECD countries, the less mobile incomes are perceived to be, the higher welfare spending.

There are two main accounts in the literature concerned with the relationship between people's expectations about their future incomes and the determinants of their attitudes toward redistribution: the "tunnel effect" (Hirschman, 1973), and the "prospect of upward mobility" (POUM) hypothesis (Bénabou and Ok, 2001).

In a seminal paper, Hirschman (1973) emphasizes the important role played by the expectations about individuals' future incomes on their attitudes toward current income differences. He argues that, in assessing whether government should reduce wealth inequalities, not

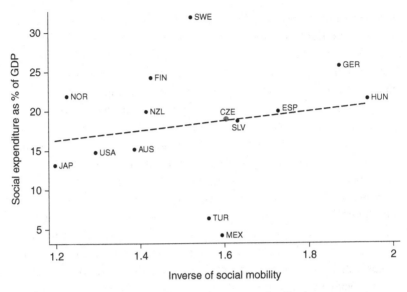

Figure 5.3. Social Mobility and Redistribution.

only do people take the status quo into account, but they also consider their prospects about future economic conditions. Poor people who view themselves on a rising income trajectory may oppose redistribution if they expect to be further up in the income ladder (and would eventually have to pay for the government's redistributive activities). Needless to say, this mechanism might also be at work in the reverse direction (i.e., the rich persons may favor redistribution because they expect to be poor sometime in the future).

Hirschman (1973) coined the term "tunnel effect" to describe this phenomenon, which explains why rising inequality may be tolerated in developing countries. The tunnel effect also explains why poor people resist lasting redistributions, and hence why we do not see more pressure for the implementation of income equalization policies in democracies where the median voter has an income below the mean.

Hirschman's contribution gave rise to a related literature analyzing the impact of the prospects of upward mobility on people's demand for redistributive policies.[6] A formal model that interprets economic

---

[6] Empirical support of Hirschman's tunnel effect is given by Ravallion and Loskin (2000), Corneo and Grüner (2000), and Alesina and La Ferrara (2001).

agents' expectations about income dynamics and justifies people's opposition to large-scale redistribution is offered by Bénabou and Ok (2001). In their model, people maximize an intertemporal utility function that takes into account expectations about the level of their future incomes. The result is similar to Hirschman's: There is a group of individuals below the average income that will oppose redistribution since they expect that their income will be above the average in the future.

It is important to note, however, that the Bénabou and Ok's argument depends on some critical assumptions. First, the redistribution scheme chosen today will last for some period of time. Second, individuals ought not to be too risk averse (i.e., they should not be too worried about changes in their relative income position). Third, some fraction of the population who is currently poorer than the average expects to be positioned above the average in the future. Finally, the income transition function needs to be concave (i.e., income will grow at a higher rate for low-income individuals). Based on these important assumptions, Bénabou and Ok derive two main results. First, the more concave the transition function of income, the smaller the share of people below average income that support redistribution. Second, this fraction of the population is smaller as the time horizon for the chosen taxation increases.

Both the tunnel effect and the POUM hypothesis reflect self-centered motives, underlying agents attitudes toward equalization policies, without any altruistic concern. The impact of social mobility on the demand for redistribution is uniquely explained by individuals' selfish calculations about their own chances and direction of mobility. It follows that, though both theories explain the impact of social mobility on people's attitudes toward redistributive taxation, they do not clarify what determines their optimistic (or pessimistic) expectations about future incomes. In other words, why do (do not) people believe in their prospects of upward mobility? Why do (do not) they trust the working of social mobility? Why do (do not) they think it is fair and just? What are the determinants of people's beliefs about the social mobility process? Can they explain cross-national differences in redistributive policies? These questions gave birth to an interdisciplinary research program whose main results we review in the next section.

5.4 DISTRIBUTIVE JUSTICE AND REDISTRIBUTION

Studies analyzing the effects of the dynamics of income on people's attitudes toward inequality have recently stressed the role of individual's perceptions about fairness in the process of social mobility. One of the earliest papers in this tradition is Piketty (1995). He argues that individuals support redistribution not only to improve their own financial situations but because of a sense of justice. In particular, redistribution should take place only to the benefit of those citizens whose low incomes are due to bad luck, rather than to those whose low incomes are due to lack of effort.

Piketty (1995) formalizes his theory through a Bayesian learning process. Each voter has a prior belief about the relative importance of effort and luck in the income-generating process. If a person believes that effort is relatively important and luck relatively unimportant, she votes for low tax rates. If she believes the opposite, low incomes must be compensated by redistributive taxation. The endogeneity of the stochastic process of belief formation, through agents' own experience about effort choices and income realizations converges to a stationary distribution of beliefs and income that affects the structure of redistributive policies.

Beliefs regarding the social and moral legitimacy of holding wealth may have an important impact on the amount of wealth leveling that a society undertakes (Putterman, 1996). These sociotropic preferences are based on the concept of "moral reciprocity" (i.e., people are willing to transfer income to others conditionally on the guarantee that the latter are not free-riding on the system).

The idea that the demand for redistribution cannot be exclusively attributed to selfish motives, but that it also depends on preferences concerning other's income and opportunities, has been empirically validated in the economic literature. Fong (2001, 2006) shows that the dynamic of income distribution and the equality of opportunities as opposed to equality of results enter in the individual's utility function. In the same vein, Alesina and La Ferrara (2001) demonstrate that a person's attitudes toward equalization policies depend on her opinions concerning the determinants of income. Individuals who think that wealth is determined by luck, social acquaintance, family history, or other similar privileges, rather than effort, education, merit, and ability, are more favorable to large redistribution. Therefore, in this perspective, individuals' view about redistributive policies may be affected by perceptions on the nature of the mobility process with a preference for the equality in opportunities rather than equality in outcomes.[7]

In order to evaluate individuals' income dynamics within a given society, scholars use subjective data collected through survey analysis. The adoption of this type of information for economic and social research is increasingly spreading. Social scientists use them to investigate the formation of utility and social interactions that are beyond the scope of the method of revealed preferences in order to guide economic policies on the basis of the expressed preferences.[8]

Evidence from ethnographic surveys conducted in United States through hundreds of detailed interviews of both white and black working-class and lower-middle-class individuals reveals the persistence of strongly motivated beliefs. More specifically, individuals cling to a belief that effort and hard work, will ultimately pay off (Lane, 1959; Rubin and Peplau, 1975; Lerner, 1982). Another important finding of the ethnographic literature is the perceived overarching importance of willpower. The key challenge in the life of the interviewed subjects is the daily struggle to keep going, to not give up, and to persevere in the face of adversity. As summarized by Lane (1959), individuals, especially the working poor, express "the general view that success is a triumph of the will and a reflection of ability" (p. 38).

A closely related perspective to account for differences in redistributive policies is proposed by Bénabou and Tirole (2006). They develop a theory that explains why people believe that the world is just and one gets what he deserves, despite the fact that the world is not so just. They borrow from recent work in psychology that deals with cognitive dissonance and stresses the possible distortions between people's perceptions and actual reality. In this context, they analyze the implications of their theory in terms of social mobility and the size of redistribution chosen by the polity.

---

[7] "People who are the most opposed to redistribution are those who believe that the social rat race is fair, that is, everyone has the same opportunities to move up in life" (Alesina and La Ferrara, 2001, p. 857).

[8] For an overview of the merits and imperfections of subjective data see Kahneman, Wakker, and Rakesh (1997), Winkelmann and Winkelmann (1998), Manski and Straub (1999), Frey and Stutzer (2002), and Ferrer-i Carbonell and Frijters (2004).

More specifically, bringing together the literature on the political economy of redistribution and that on the determinants of social mobility, they argue that, if enough individuals perceive that economic success is highly dependent on effort, they will ultimately represent a pivotal voting-block demanding low redistribution. Given the complementarity between beliefs, political outcome, and policy choice, two equilibria emerge. The first, which they call "American Equilibrium," is characterized by an optimistic belief in living in a just world that drives the process of social mobility and leads to a demand for relatively laissez-faire public policies. The second, which is defined as "European Equilibrium," is characterized by a more pessimistic view of social and economic interactions that carries with it unjust income dynamics and, in turn, a demand for a more generous welfare state.

In the same fashion, Alesina and Angeletos (2005) propose a theory that links people's attitudes toward redistribution to their view regarding the causes of wealth and poverty and the extent to which they believe themselves responsible for their own fate. Similarly to Bénabou and Tirole (2006), their model leads to the coexistence of low- and high-redistribution societies. In a recent and influential book, Alesina and Glaeser (2004) bring this perspective into the data and show that the remarkable differences in direct and indirect redistribution between the United States and Europe can be explained to a large extent by different individual beliefs concerning the fairness of the income dynamics. More specifically, they argue that in Europe the belief that birth determines status is widespread and that the poor are generally thought to be unfortunate, but not personally responsible for their own conditions. As a consequence, government intervention through extensive welfare programs is perceived as the most effective remedy to promote social mobility and to enhance the economic conditions of the poor. Differently, Americans have faith in the fact that they live in the land of opportunity where the poor have real possibilities to escape poverty out of hard work and personal responsibility.[9]

---

[9] "In America most of the rich men were formerly poor: most of those who now enjoy leisure were absorbed in business during the youth" (Tocqueville, 1951). The thirtieth American President, Calvin Coolidge, said in his 1925 inaugural address "the wise and correct course to follow in taxation and all other economic legislation is not to destroy those who have secured success but to create conditions under which everyone will have a better chance to be successful" (citations from Alesina and Glaeser 2004, 197 and 202, respectively).

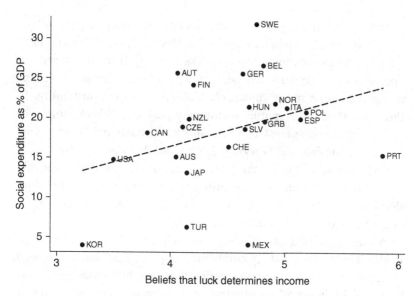

Figure 5.4. Fairness and Redistribution.

Americans, therefore, believe that they reside in a mobile society in which individual effort can lift people up the income ladder. In this context, the recourse to redistribution to reduce income inequality is significantly degraded and with it also the role of government aids as a remedy to elevate the economic conditions of the poor.

In Figure 5.4 we observe that the extent to which individuals perceive that their future economic conditions depend on luck rather than effort affects welfare spending in their country. The stronger people's belief that luck determines income, the more they live in OECD countries characterized by high welfare spending as percentage of GDP.

5.5 FURTHER MOTIVATIONS FOR REDISTRIBUTION

The literature on the determinants of redistribution and social expenditure examines also the effects of other economic, political, social, and cultural motivations that shape people's attitudes toward income inequality and opinions about the extent of the welfare state.

In an influential paper Dani Rodrik (1998) suggests that a country's large redistributive schemes can be understood as the government's response to exogenous income shocks deriving from the degree of openness of its economy. A country with a large exposure to international trade is more vulnerable to large economic instability. In this context, a larger public sector may play a stabilizing role providing insurance against external shocks through public spending. However, Alesina and Wacziarg (1998) find that country size is negatively related to government size, which, in turn, is also negatively related to trade openness. Therefore, the positive empirical relationship between openness and government size is not direct, but rather might be mediated by country size.

Alesina and Wacziarg findings, though, are not in contrast with Rodrik's ideas since, as they point out, the openness argument can well be applied to transfer programs, rather than to public goods and infrastructures. In Figure 5.5 we plot the relationship between the degree of economic openness calculated as the sum of exports and imports and the size of social expenditure both as a share of GDP. As before, the countries displayed in the figure belong to the OECD group. We note that, in line with Rodrik's theory, the relationship is positive indicating that the greater the openness of a country's economy, the higher the amount of social welfare spending.

Other relevant views on the determinants of income redistribution are linked to cultural and social aspects. Some scholars argue that different religious beliefs are associated with different economic attitudes as well as different economic outcomes. Scheve and Stasavage (2006) suggest that religion and welfare spending are substitutes in the face of adverse life events. Therefore, high religiosity in the population is associated with low redistribution and vice versa. They test this hypothesis at the individual level and find a statistically significant negative relationship between the degree of an individual religious involvement and his preference for welfare spending. In the same vein, Guiso, Sapienza, and Zingales (2003) demonstrate that the level of religiosity acts as a psychological buffer against life adversities. This again runs in favor of a positive relationship between the extent of religious beliefs and people's support for income inequality.

In Figure 5.6 we describe the relationship between welfare spending as a share of GDP and the degree of religiosity measured by the extent

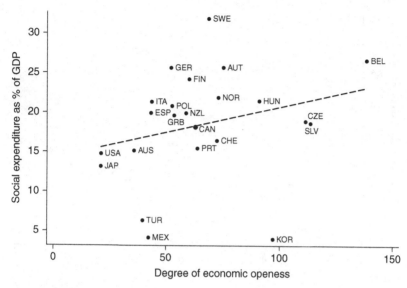

Figure 5.5. Economic Openness and Redistribution.

of self-reported church attendance. We note a clear positive relationship indicating that the greater the degree of religiosity, the higher social expenditures in OECD countries are (results do not change if we use different measures of self-reported degree of religiosity).

Drawing from a literature pioneered by Weber (2002), Bénabou and Tirole (2006) argue that people whose attitude toward the afterlife is driven by the so-called Protestant ethic are more likely to be hard workers and low supporters of redistribution. Such individuals believe that there is a hereafter in which a person's rewards and punishments are linked to the industriousness with which he conducted his lifetime. In this perspective, success is seen as a religious sign of being chosen and, therefore, as something that one should strive for.

If, on the one hand, religiosity plays a significant role as a social and cultural factor in shaping people's attitudes toward the extent of the welfare state, on the other, an important literature emerged on the effect of another social and cultural aspect that impacts on the individuals' preferences for income transfers: group fragmentation in the population along racial or ethnic lines. In the economic literature, several measures have been constructed to calculate the fragmentation in societies along racial, ethnic, linguistic, and cultural lines in order

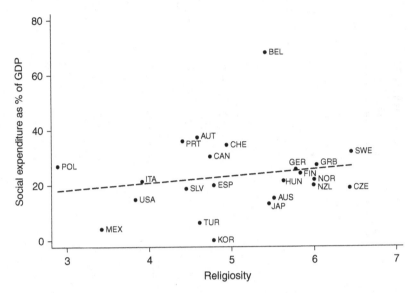

Figure 5.6. Religion and Redistribution.

to evaluate their effects on economic outcomes (Alesina et al., 2003; Fearon, 2003). In this framework, it has been argued that people of different races and of different ethnic groups look at each other with suspicion.[10] It follows that when differences in income are correlated with race, one may feel less generous in terms of welfare.

In the United States there is a considerable empirical evidence that, even controlling for income and other individual characteristics, whites are less favorable to social spending than nonwhites (Alesina and La Ferrara 2001; Fong 2001). The interpretation of this result is that white Americans feel that a large extent of welfare spending goes to minorities. Therefore, they are less prone to redistribution than they would otherwise be in a more homogeneous society. In this context, the support for income transfer is greater among people who live close to welfare recipients who by and large are of the same race (Luttmer, 2001).

In Figures 5.7 and 5.8 we plot the extent of ethnic and religious fractionalization against the size of social spending as percentage of GDP

---

[10] Experimental evidence shows that trust travels fast and smoothly within the same race (Hero, 2003; Banting et al., 2006; Bjornskov, 2006; Putnam, 2007).

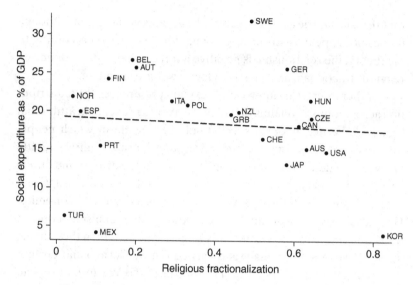

Figure 5.7. Religious Fractionalization and Redistribution.

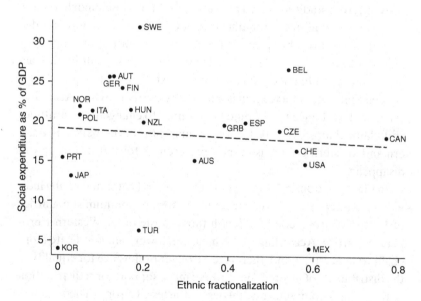

Figure 5.8. Ethnic Fractionalization and Redistribution.

for OECD countries, respectively. In both cases we note that, although it does not appear as strong as one might have expected according to the theory, the relationship is negative implying that higher ethnic and religious fractionalization leads to lower welfare spending.

Another interesting approach to explain preferences for redistribution across countries claims that they are likely to depend on attitudinal legacies inherited under a specific political regime in which people were exposed to a strong bias toward "egalitarianism." Suhrcke (2001) analyzes the determinants of people's attitudes toward income differences in postsocialist countries of Eastern and Central Europe and compares them with those in Western established market economies. He finds that, after a decade of breakdown of communism, people in transition countries are significantly more egalitarian than those living in the West. A similar analysis is carried out by Corneo and Grüner (2002). They compare six Eastern European and six Western European countries and again find that the former have stronger preferences for redistribution than the latter.

A different study is offered by Alesina and Fuchs-Schündeln (2007). They show that after the reunification of Germany, East Germans displayed more favorable preferences toward redistribution than their fellow citizens in West Germany. They explain this result by the fact that, after about half a century of communist dictatorship, people still believe that state intervention is a necessity for their living. Also, they calculate how long a time would be required to change these attitudes and claim that, in twenty to forty years, differences between Eastern and Western Germans in their preferences for redistribution will disappear.

In Figures 5.9 and 5.10 we report Suhrcke's indicator measuring individuals' preferences for redistribution in former communist countries of Eastern Europe compared with those in the other Western European countries. According to this measure, lower values indicate more egalitarian attitudes and, therefore, stronger preference for equality in the distribution of income. We observe more support for redistribution in the former communist countries of Eastern Europe. These results are evidence of an attitudinal legacy inherited from socialist times in which people were exposed to a strong bias towards egalitarianism.

Keeping the political argument alive, we ought to dedicate a final remark to those studies that associate the extent of welfare spending to

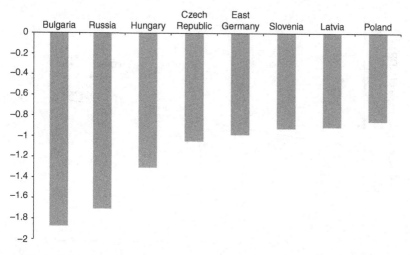

Figure 5.9. Individual Preferences for Redistribution in Former Communist Countries.

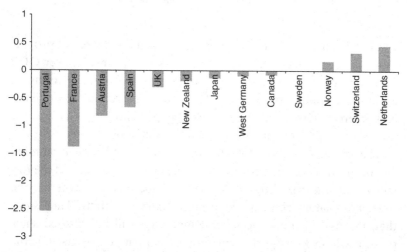

Figure 5.10. Individual Preferences for Redistribution in Western Europe.

the working of political institutions. In particular, we refer to the work of several economists and political scientists who point out that proportional systems of representation – those in which many parties, even small parties, get represented in the legislature – tend to produce more redistributive spending. Their researches document, theoretically and

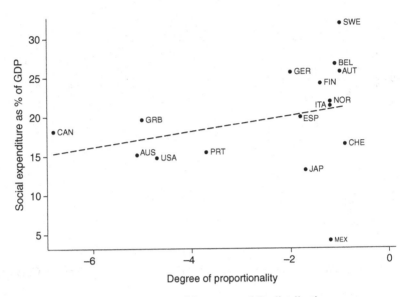

Figure 5.11. Electoral Systems and Redistribution.

empirically, a very strong correlation between the degree of proportionality of the electoral system and the size of transfers over GDP (Persson and Tabellini 2000; Milesi-Ferretti, Perotti, and Rostagno, 2002; Lizzeri and Persico, 2001). These findings are plotted in Figure 5.11 where welfare spending increases, in percentage of GDP, as the degree of proportionality in the electoral system rises.

The argument goes as follows. They distinguish between plurality and proportional electoral systems on the basis of the fact that the former are characterized by small single-member districts, whereas the latter are characterized by large multimember districts. They show that, in large districts, electoral competition will be diffused since parties will seek support from broad coalitions of voters. On the contrary, in small districts, competition will be concentrated in geographically determined constituencies and spending will be targeted locally. Thus, when the district magnitude is large, public expenditures will be broad and composed principally of income transfers, whereas when it is small expenditure will be mainly composed of local public goods.

There is another explanation that links proportional representation systems to higher welfare spending. This is based on the fact that Parliaments elected under proportionality are usually very fragmented. Political fragmentation leads to the formation of multiparty coalition governments that are instrumental for large and more persistent public deficits (Roubini and Sachs, 1989; Alesina and Drazen, 1991).

5.6 CONCLUDING REMARKS

The literature overview presented in this chapter started with a redistribution paradox: Why in modern democracies do not the relatively poor majority use their votes to impose large-scale redistributions by extensive expropriations of income from the rich? This paradox triggered the interest of many scholars on the economics and politics of redistribution. This literature not only examined the determinants of the extent of redistribution but also focused on the causes that lead different countries to support different sizes of the welfare state.

The main message of this literature is that subjective beliefs matter since they shape people's perceptions about the determinants of income differentials and, as a consequence, people's attitudes toward inequality and their opinion about the role of the welfare state. More specifically, redistribution policies have been presented as the result of an endogenous process of belief formation through the individuals' own experience with effort choices and income realizations.

In the next chapter, we link individuals' perception about the determinants of income differentials with the concept of autonomy freedom described in the first part of this book. Our aim is to argue that the more autonomous an individual is, the higher her perception of being in control over her own choices and the stronger her feeling that how her life turns out is her responsibility. Such responsibility over her own life outcomes affects her opinion about whether the working of the process of social mobility is just and, therefore, her demand for redistribution.

6

Autonomy Freedom and Redistribution

6.1 INTRODUCTION

Income inequality is one of the crucial problems associated with the capitalist model of economic organization, since it is an unescapable and largely disapproved consequence of capitalism. Since capitalism allows for inequality – so goes the received wisdom – then it is important to put in place mechanisms to control it. However, international surveys show remarkable differences in the ways inequality is perceived across countries. These surveys cast doubt on how general the received wisdom is and suggest that simplistic redistributive policies are unlikely to be optimal. In this chapter, we analyze the determinants of people's preferences toward income redistribution and their economic consequences. In particular, we argue that individuals' attitudes toward redistribution depend upon the extent of freedom people enjoy.

Despite the effort devoted to the analysis of individuals' preferences for redistribution, freedom has never been conceived as a potential driver in shaping these preferences. Yet, as we argue in this chapter, freedom is a key causal antecedent of people's preferences toward redistribution. Recognition of the role of freedom is therefore crucial in designing optimal redistributive policies.

The sense in which freedom sheds light on individuals' preferences for redistribution can be illustrated by considering their trade-off with social mobility: The greater the perception that individuals are mobile

This chapter has been written in collaboration with Dario Maimone Ansaldo Patti.

in society, the lesser the preference for flattening income differences through redistributive schemes (Piketty, 1995). However, this trade-off is qualified by the perceived fairness of the process through which social mobility occurs namely, the extent to which outcomes are under a person's volitional control rather than be dependent upon privileges given by third-party interventions or luck. Where individuals perceive "unfair advantages" that unduly affect their position on the income ladder, they favor redistribution through public policy as a corrective tool. "[T]he belief on whether the mobility process is 'fair' or on whether society offers equal opportunities to its members may be an important determinant of the demand for redistribution" (Alesina and La Ferrara, 2005, p. 898).

The crucial role of freedom becomes apparent here. As Alesina and Angeletos (2005) point out, "[e]ndogeneizing the concept of fairness, and understanding why societies consider some sources of inequality justifiable and others unfair" (p. 971), is an important exercise still to be accomplished. Freedom sheds light just on the process that shapes individuals' perceptions of fairness. Consider the concept, central to this book, of autonomy freedom. We already pointed out, in Chapter 4, that people who enjoy autonomy freedom have, to a large extent, control over their achievements. Therefore, what they perceive as fair or unfair is likely to depend upon the degree of autonomy freedom they enjoy. Being in control of their own achievements, people with high levels of autonomy freedom are likely to perceive the game in life as a fair process where individual skills and abilities dominate luck and privileges of any sort. On the contrary, people with low levels of autonomy freedom are likely to perceive economic and social outcomes as largely dependent upon elements outside their own control. Ceteris paribus, the former group are less likely to favor the use of redistribution as a corrective tool for the unfairness of life. Autonomy freedom is then primitive in the causal link between the tolerance for inequality and preferences regarding redistribution. As such, it is a cornerstone for the analysis of redistributive policies.

In this chapter, we use the concept of autonomy freedom introduced in Chapter 3 to explain people's attitudes toward income redistribution and assess their policy impact. We construct a model in which we describe the effects of an individual's level of autonomy freedom on her preferences for redistribution and her willingness to work. To validate our theory, we test the predictions of our model by using the empirical measure of autonomy freedom presented in Chapter 4.

6.2 AUTONOMY FREEDOM AND TASTE FOR REDISTRIBUTION

Some Preliminary Concepts

In the literature reviewed in Chapter 5 we observed that a relevant amount of research on the determinants of redistribution and welfare spending considers people's beliefs about fairness in social processes as an important explanation for individual attitudes toward inequality and preference for income transfers. But how is it that some people view some sources of inequality justifiable and others unfair? One answer is autonomy freedom. Autonomous individuals perceive achievements as fair if they believe that what they attain in life depends on their choices (i.e., their life outcomes are largely determined by what they choose and how they act, Bavetta et al., 2008).

The role that autonomy freedom plays here is made possible by its relationship with achievements. Autonomous individuals are engaged in a conscious decision process through which they select the preference relation that they use to make their choice. Since their decision process relies upon their personal and moral qualities, autonomous individuals are likely to perceive themselves as being responsible for successes and failures experienced in their life since whatever outcome they attain is connected to their choices. This is a point that we have forcefully defended in Chapter 4.

The relationship between autonomy freedom and achievements that we have proposed can also be defended in the light of some empirical regularities put forward by an interdisciplinary set of studies. Many theories in social psychology, in human resource management, and in economics suggest that autonomy is directly connected with intrinsic motivations and performance (Deci and Flaste, 1995; Frey, 1997; Deci, Koestner, and Ryan, 1999; Sansone and Harackiewicz, 2000). In these studies, autonomy is never equated with independence or individualism, but rather with a sense of internal self-control that shapes the development of a person's individuality (Deci and Ryan, 1985). Research analyzing the impact of freedom and autonomy in individual and team productivity shows that personal development, self-determination, and responsibility are crucial factors in improving work effort and performance (Eisenberger, Rhoades, and Cameron, 1999; Langfred, 2005; Mudambi, Mudambi, and Navarra, 2007; Falk and Kosfeld, 2006). Therefore, given the relationship between Millian autonomy and performance, on the one hand, and performance and achievements on the other, we can hypothesize that an individual's autonomy freedom is also linked with the control he exerts over his achievements.

The observed empirical regularities reinforce the link between autonomy freedom and achievements. It follows that autonomous individuals, holding themselves responsible over the way their lives turn out, perceive themselves to be in control of their own actions. This implies an important causal relationship between the development of a person's autonomy freedom and the perception of the self as the real master of his own destiny.

Another important aspect that deserves to be noted concerns the fact that the notion of autonomy freedom casts light upon the concept of fairness individuals rely upon in shaping their preferences for redistribution. According to Frey, Benz, and Stutzer (2004), social mobility may be interpreted in procedural terms: If people believe that society offers equal opportunities through actual income mobility, they may be less concerned with inequality because they see social processes as fair. In this perspective, it is the noninstrumental pleasures and displeasures of the process that are valued by individuals, rather than the actual outcomes that they achieve. In light of these results, if individuals perceive themselves as autonomous agents who determine their economic status, they feel that the mobility process is fair since equal opportunities exist. In contrast, those who perceive that income dynamics in society is not determined by the choices of autonomous people, see social mobility as a biased process in which mobility opportunities are exploited only by some and not by all.

Besides providing a theoretical foundation to preferences for redistribution, autonomy freedom sheds further light upon the economic analysis of redistributive policies. As highlighted in Chapter 5, the literature suggests that preferences for redistribution are affected by the racial composition of a society: People do not like to give their money to individuals who have not the same skin color so, where ethnic fragmentation prevails, redistribution is lower (Alesina, Glaeser, and Sacerdote, 2001; Alesina and Glaeser, 2004). But autonomy freedom allows a more fine-grained analysis: Rather than looking at race or ethnic characteristics, it enables us to focus on whether people retain control of their lives independently of any other distinctive feature. Preferences for redistributive policies would therefore depend on individual rather than group characteristics. Recognition of such intragroup preference heterogeneity allows for more efficient policy design.

The arguments discussed so far lead to straightforward implications for the relationship between autonomy freedom and preferences for redistribution. Individuals who enjoy high levels of autonomy freedom value income differences more than those whose degree of autonomy freedom is low and, therefore, are less likely to support redistributive taxation schemes.

The Theoretical Model

In this section we analyze the relationship between the level of autonomy freedom perceived by an individual and her preference for income transfers.

We construct a simple labor–leisure trade-off model in which an individual sequentially expresses her optimal preference for income transfers and sets accordingly the amount of effort to unfold in her work activities. Unlike other studies where the level of the individual's effort affects her preferred level of income transfers (Alesina, Glaeser, and Sacerdote, 2001), in our model we are interested in analyzing the effect of transfers on the level of effort selected by the individual. Our choice, which is in line with important theoretical and empirical contribution in the literature (Murphy, Shleifer, and Vishny, 1991; La Porta et al., 1999), aims at examining whether the level of transfers chosen by the individual leads her to carry out either a productive or a rent-seeking behavior.

The individual seeks to maximize the following quasi-linear utility function:

$$U = y^N + \log(l) \tag{6.1}$$

where l is the amount of leisure and y^N the individual's net income which is given by:

$$y^N = y + S \tag{6.2}$$

where y is the amount of income raised by the individual and S the income transfer.

In our model, there are three sources of income: income due to work effort, e, to environmental factors, v, and to past income, W. In the income generation process, work effort is the individual's choice variable since it is under her control. The relationship between work effort and income is intuitive (i.e., greater work effort leads to higher income). The environmental factors are those events that, although they fall outside the individual's control, affect her ability to produce income. A large win at the lottery or being born in a wealthy family are two examples of environmental factors that affect the level of the individual's income directly and indirectly, respectively. As such, environmental factors can be considered as a random component in the individual's income generation process. Better outcomes with regard to environmental factors (for example, a win at the lottery) lead to higher levels of income.

Following a methodology proposed by Alesina, Glaeser, and Sacerdote (2001), the labor–leisure decision in past periods is not modeled. Therefore, the level of W enters the model exogenously.

Taking into consideration the three sources of income, we have:

$$y = \theta \left[\alpha e + (1 - \alpha) v \right] + (1 - \theta) W \tag{6.3}$$

where $\theta \in [0,1]$ parametrizes income mobility. Low values of θ indicate a high level of income persistence. Conversely, high values of θ indicate a low level of income persistence. In the former case, work efforts carried out in the past and past environmental factors have a strong effect on current income, whereas in the latter case the opposite applies. The level of autonomy freedom is captured by $\alpha \in [0,1]$ whose value measures the relative impact of effort and environmental factors on the production of income as perceived by the individual.

As mentioned, we posit a relationship between an individual's level of autonomy freedom and her perception of the extent to which income generation is under her control. The higher the control of the individual over the determinants of her income is, the greater her autonomy freedom will be. Therefore, a greater α indicates higher levels of autonomy freedom since, in the production of the individual's income, work effort – a variable under the individual's volitional control – is perceived more effective than environmental factors – the random component in the income generating process. Differently, a smaller α signals low levels of autonomy freedom since environmental factors are considered more effective than work effort in generating income.

As far as income transfer is concerned, we hypothesize that the individual's desired level of transfers S is given by her preferences for income transfers, t, and her level of income, y, as compared to the average income in society, M. Such a desired amount of transfers may be either positive or negative depending on whether y is either lower or higher than M. More specifically, we have:

$$S = t(M - y) \tag{6.4}$$

Substituting (6.3) and (6.4) into (6.2), we may derive the following explicit equation for the individual's net income:

$$y^N = (1 - t)\{\theta[\alpha e + (1 - \alpha)v] + (1 - \theta)W\} + tM \tag{6.5}$$

The individual seeks to maximize the utility function in (6.1) subject to the following time constraint:

$$T = e + l \tag{6.6}$$

where T is the total time available.

Before proceeding with the maximization problem, it is important to note that v is uniformly distributed over the interval $[0, T]$. Such a distribution of v brings about two important effects that deserve to be noted. First, $E(v) > 0$ and $(T - v) \geq 0$, which imply that some components of the individual's environment are nonstochastic (e.g., personal connections), whereas others are stochastic (e.g., winning at the lottery). Second, the individual's income is always strictly lower than the average income in society ($M > R$) when she does not unfold any effort in her work activities and the environmental factors are not beneficial to her.

Let us now move to the individual's maximization problem. As already pointed out, the individual's maximization is carried out sequentially: She first chooses her optimal preference for income transfers and, then, the amount of effort to unfold in her work activities. We solve the model backward and, therefore, begin by deriving the optimal level of effort, taking as fixed the individual's preference for transfers.

Using the time constraint, we may rewrite the individual's income as follows:

$$y^N = (1-t)\{\theta[\alpha(T-l)+(1-\alpha)v]+(1-\theta)W\}+tM \qquad (6.7)$$

Substituting equation (6.7) into the utility function, the constrained maximization problem reduces in choosing the optimal level of leisure:

$$\max_l U = (1-t)\{\theta[\alpha(T-l)+(1-\alpha)v]+(1-\theta)W\}+tM+\log l$$

$$(6.8)$$

Maximization yields the following values for work effort, e, and leisure, l, in terms of the individual's preference for income transfers, t, the level of perceived autonomy freedom, α, and the extent of income mobility, θ:

$$l(t,\alpha,\theta) = \frac{1}{1-t\theta\alpha} \qquad (6.9)$$

$$e(t,\alpha,\theta) = \frac{T(1-t\theta\alpha)-1}{1-t\theta\alpha} \qquad (6.10)$$

We can now move backward to calculate the individual's optimal income transfers. Substituting (6.10) into equation (6.4), which characterizes the desired level of transfers, we obtain:

$$\max_t S = t\left\{M-\left[\theta\left(\alpha\frac{T(1-t\theta\alpha)-1}{1-t\theta\alpha}+(1-\alpha)v\right)+(1-\theta)W\right]\right\}$$

$$(6.11)$$

The equilibrium value for t is the solution to the following first-order condition:

$$(1-t\theta\alpha)^2\{M-W(1-\theta)-\theta[T\alpha+v(1-\alpha)]\}+\theta\alpha = 0 \qquad (6.12)$$

Using the equilibrium value t^*, we may define e^* and l^* which solve the model.

The Comparative Statics

Although the model cannot be solved explicitly, we can evaluate how the main parameters of the model affect the optimal choices of transfers, t^*, and of work effort, e^*. This allows us to address the following questions:

1. What is the relationship between the individual level of autonomy freedom and her optimal preference for income transfers?
2. What is the relationship between the individual level of autonomy freedom and the extent of work effort in the income generation process?

We start our comparative statics analysis by focusing on the relationship between an individual level of autonomy freedom and her optimal preference for transfers, t^*, and effort, e^*. Proposition 6.1 describes the result that we obtain.

Proposition 6.1 *The higher the individual's level of autonomy freedom, the lower her preferences for income transfers and the higher the effort she unfolds in the income generation process.*

The negative relationship between the individual's level of autonomy freedom and her optimal choice of income transfers can be explained in light of the concept of procedural utility whereby individuals value conditions and processes that lead to economic outcomes rather than economic outcomes per se (Frey, Benz, and Stutzer, 2004). In this framework, income inequality is not evaluated per se, but it is judged with respect to the processes that brings it about. If an individual believes that she is in control over her actions, she considers herself to be master of her own destiny and, therefore, willing to affect her own income level. In this case, the individual, owing to a concept of procedural fairness applied at the personal level, believes that whatever her economic conditions are, they are deserved. The importance that the individual attaches to procedural fairness leads to her opposition to any form of transfer, no matter whether she is (or is not) the recipient.

This concept of procedural fairness applied at the personal level has consequences at the aggregate level on the relationship between society's autonomy freedom and its preference for redistributive policies. The larger the number of autonomous individuals in society, the greater its aggregate autonomy freedom and the lower its support for redistribution. On the contrary, the smaller the number of autonomous individuals, the lower aggregate autonomy freedom and the higher societal support for redistribution. These implications at the aggregate level will be investigated in the next chapter.

As far as the relationship between the individual's level of autonomy freedom and effort is concerned, this relationship is both direct and indirect. The direct effect is explained by the fact that since autonomous individuals are masters of their own destiny, they also believe that the way their lives turn out depends on the amount of effort and commitment they are willing to produce in their work activities. The indirect effect works through the negative relationship between the individual's preference for income transfers and her level of autonomy freedom. The higher the individual's level of autonomy freedom, the lower her preference for transfers and the higher her work effort. This is because highly autonomous individuals do not support income transfers and, therefore, are aware that their economic conditions depend on hard work and commitment.

Let us now move on to the analysis of the effect of the degree of income mobility perceived by the individual, θ, and the equilibrium values of income transfers, t^*, and effort, e^*. Proposition 6.2 describes our result.

Proposition 6.2 *The higher the degree of income mobility perceived by the individual, the lower her preferences for income transfers and the higher the effort she unfolds in the income generation process.*

This finding is in line with that part of the literature that links people's preference for transfers with future income dynamics (Hirschman, 1973; Bénabou and Ok, 2001; Alesina and La Ferrara, 2005). Individuals who think that they live in a mobile society where chances to enhance economic conditions are greater, are more likely to oppose income transfers, for purely self-centered motivations. Further, highly mobile societies are also conducive to greater effort and commitment since individuals are more likely to believe that hard work pays (Piketty, 1995; Bénabou and Tirole, 2006; Fong, 2006).

Finally, our theoretical model allows us to examine the effect exercised by the level of the average income in society and the equilibrium values of income transfers, t^*, and effort, e^*. Proposition 6.3 describes our result.

Proposition 6.3 *The higher the average income in the society, the higher an individual's preference for income transfers, and the lower the effort she unfolds in the income generation process.*

This result can be understood in light of the fact that, given the income of the individual, the higher the difference between her income and the average income level in society, the greater her demand for income transfers (Ravallion and Loskin, 2000; Corneo and Grüner, 2000). Greater transfers require high tax rates to be financed. According to a large empirical labor supply literature, the latter have unfavorable effects on the level of effort that the individuals carry out in their work activities (Prescott, 2006). Thus, we have the negative relationship between preferences for income transfers and work effort in the income generation process.

6.3 THE DATA

We use data from the World Value Survey database to test the validity of our model's predictions. We analyze the OECD countries over a time span that covers the years 1989–1999. Summary statistics and the correlation matrix are shown in Tables 6.1 and 6.2.

Let us now describe each variable used in the empirical analysis in more detail starting with the two dependent variables and later moving to the three primary independent variables and the controls.

The Individual's Choice Variables

The individual decision process is structured in two stages. As a consequence, we have two dependent choice variables in our study. The first concerns the individual's transfer decision and, therefore, indicates her preferences for redistribution. We proxy these preferences by the individual's answer to the following question:

How would you place your views on this scale? 1 means that you agree completely with the statement that *we need large income differences*; 10 means that you completely agree with the statement that *incomes should be made more equal*; if your views fall somewhere in between, you can choose any number in between.

Respondents faced a ten-point scale in which the two extremes, 1 and 10, are defined in the question. From the construction of the question, each individual's taste for income transfer is ordered in a descending fashion: High values indicate high preferences for transfers and vice versa. Several studies that examine the determinants of

Table 6.1. *Summary Statistics*

Variable	Obs	Mean	SD	Min	Max
Effort vs Luck	44852	4.301547	3.00728	1	10
Preferences for Income Transfers 1	44852	5.882436	3.336658	1	10
Preferences for Income Transfers 2	44508	6.406781	3.110224	1	10
Autonomy Freedom	44852	6.532975	2.591322	1	10
Gender	44810	0.4904932	0.4999152	0	1
Age	44770	40.68365	15.71278	15	94
Income Mobility (ϑ)	44852	1.595737	0.4907543	1	2
Education	43331	1.926842	0.7309404	1	3
Single	44779	0.2239443	0.4168898	0	1
Married	44779	0.6070256	0.4884167	0	1
Religiosity	44016	2.134451	1.070123	1	4
Health Status	44754	2.324999	0.9382648	1	5
Trust	43363	1.751355	0.4322326	1	2
Difference from Median Income	38985	0.2330896	2.375166	−6	8
Self-Reported Income	38985	4.438117	2.564352	1	10
Paid-Employed	42849	0.3937081	0.4885771	0	1
Self-Employed	42849	0.0884268	0.2839179	0	1
Political Orientation	36275	5.62572	2.366962	1	10
Transtition Countries	44852	0.3973959	0.4893646	0	1

Source: World Values Survey (2009).

individuals' attitudes toward inequality in either a single country or in a crosssection of countries have used similar survey measures for assessing individuals' tastes for income redistribution (see, for example, Ravallion and Loskin, 2000; Suhrcke, 2001; Fong, 2001; Corneo and Grüner, 2002; Ohtake and Tomioka, 2004). It is important to note, however, that our dataset is the largest in terms of countries considered as well as people interviewed.

Table 6.2. Correlation Matrix

Variables	1	2	3	4	5	6	7	8	9	10	11	12	13	14	15	16	17	18	19
1 Effort vs Luck	1																		
2 Preferences for Income Transfers 1	0.0064	1																	
3 Preferences for Income Transfers 2	0.0041	−0.1884*	1																
4 Autonomy Freedom	−0.0493*	0.0898*	−0.1402*	1															
5 Gender	−0.0464*	0.0217*	−0.0310*	0.0449*	1														
6 Age	−0.0351*	−0.0643*	0.0522*	−0.0661*	0.0011	1													
7 Income Mobility (ϑ)	0.1341*	−0.0406*	0.1565*	−0.1357*	−0.0524*	0.0507*	1												
8 Education	0.0073	0.1787*	−0.0860*	0.0938*	0.0272*	−0.2177*	−0.0283*	1											
9 Single	0.0119	0.0308*	−0.0170*	0.0650*	0.0581*	−0.4803*	−0.0287*	0.1364*	1										
10 Married	−0.0395*	0.0082	0.0038	−0.0427*	0.0562*	0.2417*	−0.0085	−0.0484*	−0.6676*	1									

	1	2	3	4	5	6	7	8	9	10	11	12	13	14	15	16	17	18	19
11 Religiosity	0.1154*	−0.0228*	0.0157*	−0.0055	0.1033*	−0.0145*	0.0468*	0.0795*	−0.0025	−0.0175*	1								
12 Health Status	0.0431*	−0.0280*	0.1276*	−0.2135*	−0.0736*	0.3021*	0.1352*	−0.1495*	−0.1617*	0.0574*	−0.0109	1							
13 Trust	0.0121	0.0426*	0.0459*	−0.0440*	−0.012	−0.0298*	0.0729*	−0.0631*	0.0168*	−0.0087	−0.1104*	0.0840*	1						
14 Difference from Median Income	−0.0117	0.1367*	−0.0980*	0.1135*	0.0640*	−0.1644*	−0.0576*	0.3154*	0.0328*	0.0884*	0.0747*	−0.1687*	−0.0302*	1					
15 Self-Reported Income	0.0101	0.1056*	−0.1130*	0.1133*	0.0575*	−0.0994*	−0.0617*	0.3121*	−0.0025	0.1072*	0.1763*	−0.1668*	−0.0953*	0.8604*	1				
16 Paid-Employed	0.0252*	0.0526*	−0.0261*	0.0383*	0.1570*	−0.1202*	−0.0181*	0.1883*	−0.0694*	0.0995*	0.1562*	−0.0958*	−0.0429*	0.2056*	0.2089*	1			
17 Self-Employed	−0.0452*	0.0356*	−0.0232*	0.0342*	0.1323*	−0.0344*	−0.0398*	−0.0496*	−0.0444*	0.0604*	0.0604*	−0.0491*	0.0173*	0.0200*	0.0213*	−0.2510*	1		
18 Political Orientation	−0.0566*	0.1323*	−0.1096*	0.0763*	0.0109	−0.0079	−0.1150*	−0.005	0.0096	0.0085	−0.1460*	−0.0561*	0.0202*	0.0267*	0.0105	−0.0347*	0.0477*	1	
19 Transition Countries	0.0538*	0.0811*	0.1905*	−0.1735*	−0.0276*	0.0785*	0.1179*	0.0580*	−0.0717*	0.0650*	0.2153*	0.2009*	−0.0068	−0.0235*	−0.0537*	0.1071*	−0.0917*	−0.0622*	1

Note: '*' denotes significance at 1% level.
Source: World Values Survey (2009).

135

The second choice variable is concerned with the individual's effort decision and, therefore, indicates the amount of effort that a respondent is willing to carry out in her work activities. We proxy the individual's effort decision with a four-point scale variable whose values are ordered in descending fashion as follows: high values indicate that work is not important and low values indicate that work is important. Therefore, high values of the variable show high preferences for effort and vice versa.

The Primary Independent Variables

Propositions 6.1 to 6.3 indicate that the individual's optimal levels of transfers and effort are affected by three main variables: autonomy freedom, the perception about the extent of income mobility, and the average income held in society. These are the primary independent variables that will be used in the empirical investigation.

The empirical measure of an individual's level of autonomy freedom is introduced in Chapter 4. It is constructed on answers to the following question:

Some people feel they have completely free choice and control over their lives, while other people feel that what they do has no real effect on what happens to them. Please use this ten-point scale in which 1 means *none at all*, and 10 means *a great deal* to indicate *how much freedom of choice and control you feel you have over the way your life turns out*.

Recall that the question posed in the WVS contains both aspects of the notion of autonomy freedom discussed in Chapter 3. On the one hand, information about the number of available options is given by that part of the question where the respondent is asked to assess how much freedom of choice she enjoys. On the other hand, information about the individual's awareness of his own choices emerges in that part of the question in which the respondent is asked how much control she perceives over life outcomes (see Chapter 4 for a discussion of the empirical measure of autonomy freedom).

In line with similar variables used in other studies (Alesina and Glaeser, 2004), the individual's perception of income mobility is measured by her answer to the following question:

In your opinion, do most poor people in this country have a *chance of escaping from poverty*, or is there very little of chance escaping?

The variable is a binary dummy, which takes value 1 if the respondent believes that there is little chance for poor people to escape poverty and value 0 if the respondent believes that people have a chance to escape poverty. If the individual believes that people have chances to work their way out of poverty, it is reasonable to hypothesize that she thinks there is income mobility in the community where she lives. The opposite applies if she believes that the poor have little chances to escape poverty.

Finally, our last primary independent variable is the average income held by the individual in the society where she lives. This gives a proxy of the individual's net loss from redistribution (Roberts, 1977). As we work with survey data, we do not have the possibility of calculating the average societal income unless we carry out this computation using the self-reported information. However, as doubts exist on the methodology's reliability, we eliminate the average income level in society from our empirical analysis.

Other Independent Variables

Several other independent variables are included in the dataset employed for our empirical investigation. They range from sociodemographic variables to individuals' opinions about politics, religion, and society.

As far as the socioeconomic variables are concerned, to capture the effect of income on the individuals' preference for redistribution we consider the level of self-reported income. Respondents were asked to express the level of their income on a ten-point scale with low and high values indicating low and high levels of income, respectively. A binary dummy variable is used to indicate the gender of respondents. It takes value 1 if the respondent is male and 0 if female. Age is expressed in years. The education level is computed on a three-point scale in ascending order, from low to high levels of education. The marital status of respondents is captured by two dummies indicating whether she is either single (0) or married (1). We also construct a variable that measures the difference between the respondent's self-reported income and the median self-reported income in society calculated at the country level. Positive values indicate that the individual's self-reported income is higher than the median self-reported income in society and vice versa. The respondent's employment status is described by two dummy variables according to whether she is a paid employee (1) or is self-employed (0). Since the individual's preferences for effort might be affected by her health conditions, we included a variable referring to the health status of respondents. Such a variable is ordered on a five-point scale ranging from 1 (very good health status) to 5 (very poor health status).

The variables measuring people attitudes toward politics, religion, and society are the following. The respondent's political opinion is measured over a ten-point scale whose values 1 and 10 indicate extreme left and extreme right political orientation, respectively. The individual's opinion about whether to trust others is measured by a binary dummy variable whose value is 1 if she believes that people should be trusted and 2 otherwise. The respondent's religiosity is indicated by her assessment of whether religion is important in life. The variable is coded in descending order over a four-point range with the two extreme values, 1 and 4, indicating that religion is very important and not at all important, respectively.

Finally, to account for the effect that living in a former communist country may have on the individual's preferences for income transfers, we include a dummy variable that takes the value 1 if the country of the respondent is a transition economy and 0 otherwise.

6.4 THE EMPIRICAL METHODOLOGY

In the previous section we modeled the effect of an individual's level of autonomy freedom on her optimal transfer and effort decisions in a two-stage decision process. In the first stage she makes her *transfers decision* by expressing her optimal level of income transfers, whereas in the second stage she makes her *effort decision* by selecting accordingly how much effort to unfold in her work activities. Our main result is that higher autonomy freedom leads to lower transfers and higher effort (Proposition 6.1). We also found that income mobility and average income affect both optimal income transfers and work effort (Propositions 6.2 and 6.3). In the empirical model that follows, we implement a strategy to test the theoretical predictions stated in Propositions 6.1 and 6.2 only. As already mentioned, Proposition 6.3 is not empirically tested due to lack of reliable data.

In the empirical model, both the transfer and the effort decisions are modeled accordingly with the two dependent variables defined in the data section. In the first stage, individuals choose their most preferred level of transfers on the basis of a ten-point scale going from low to high transfers. Such a scale has been divided in two different parts each indicating low and high transfers, respectively. More specifically, the individual's preferences for transfers are low when the values on the scale range between 1 and 4 and high when they range between 7 and 10. Similarly, in the second stage, individuals choose their most preferred level of work effort on the basis of a ten-point scale going from high to low work efforts. As before, the effort scale has been divided in two parts each indicating low and high work effort, respectively. More specifically, the individual's preferences for effort are low when the value on the scale is between 7 and 10 and high when it is between 1 and 4.

To test empirically the theoretical predictions of our model we construct a two-stage decision tree as depicted in Figures 6.1 and 6.2. In both figures the first stage describes the transfer decision while the second stage refers to the effort decision. In Figure 6.1 we focus on those individuals who choose high transfers in the first stage and low effort in the second (see the thick lines in the figure). Differently, in Figure 6.2 we concentrate on those individuals who choose low transfers in the first stage and high effort in the second (see the thick lines in the figure). In the empirical part of this paper our objective is to estimate the probability that autonomy freedom and income mobility affect the decision process as described in Figures 6.1 and 6.2 in the way indicated by Propositions 6.1 and 6.2.

We use two different econometric procedures to estimate the two models depicted in Figures 6.1 and 6.2: the conditional logit (CL) and the nested logit (NL) model. These two procedures are quite similar, with the CL being a special case of the NL. In the first stage of her decision process, the individual chooses a transfer level $t \in n$, where n is the number of available transfer alternatives. Similarly, in the second stage, she chooses the level of effort $e \in m$, where m is the available number of effort alternatives. Let us now define two vectors

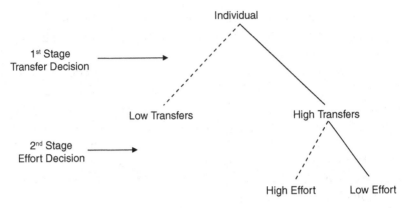

Figure 6.1. Nested Structure of the Individual's Decision Process (Model 1).

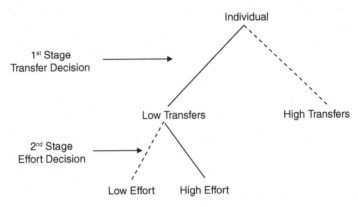

Figure 6.2. Nested Structure of the Individual's Decision Process (Model 2).

of variables, respectively $\mathbf{x}_{te}$ and $\mathbf{z}_t$, which are specific to the transfers and effort (t,e) and only transfers (t) categories, respectively. The nested logit estimator allows us to calculate the probability that an individual chooses a precise combination of transfer (t) and effort (e) on the basis of the effects exercised on her decision process by the vectors of variables as indicated by the theoretical model. For example, in Figure 6.1 (6.2), we estimate the probability that an individual chooses the combination of high (low) transfers and low (high) effort on the basis of the effect carried out on her decision process by autonomy freedom and income mobility as predicted by the comparative statics of the theoretical model (Propositions 6.1 and 6.2).

More specifically, in our empirical analysis, we estimate the following probability:

$$\Pr_{te} = \Pr_{e|t} \times \Pr_t \tag{6.13}$$

Note that the first term in equation (6.13), which is the conditional probability, is calculated by making use of the vector of regressors $\mathbf{x}_{te}$ only, according to the following expression:

$$\Pr_{e|t} = \frac{\exp(\mathbf{x}_{te}\beta)}{\sum_n \exp(\mathbf{x}_{tn}\beta)} \tag{6.14}$$

where β is a vector of parameters.

The second term in equation (6.13) is calculated by using the vector of regressors $\mathbf{z}_t$ as well as the inclusive values of category (e) which links the choice operated by the individual at the second stage to the choice he took in the first stage of the decision process. The inclusive values of category (t,e) are defined as follows:

$$I_t = \ln \left\{ \sum_n \exp(\mathbf{x}_{tn}\beta) \right\}$$

which can be used to obtain the following probability for the first stage of the decision process:

$$\Pr_t = \frac{\exp(\mathbf{z}_t\gamma + \eta_t I_t)}{\sum_m \exp(\mathbf{z}_{tm}\gamma + \eta_{tm} I_{tm})} \tag{6.15}$$

It is interesting to note that, if the inclusive parameters are all equal to unity, the equation (6.13) reduces to the probability of the conditional logit:

$$\Pr_{te} = \frac{U_{te}}{\sum_n \sum_m \exp U_{te}}$$

with $U_{te} = \mathbf{x}_{te}\beta + \mathbf{z}_t\gamma$.

Clearly, the inclusive values indicate whether a choice is nested into another. Therefore, they are crucial for checking whether the NL procedure fits the estimation of our model better than the CL. We check whether the NL procedure is preferable to the CL procedure by running a test for the independence of irrelevant alternatives (Hausman and McFadden, 1984). This test is based on the idea that if a subset of the choice set is irrelevant with respect to the other alternative, then its inclusion among the regressors does not lead to inconsistency in the estimation of the parameters of the model. The NL model (6.13) is fitted using a full-information-maximum-likelihood estimation.

6.5 ESTIMATION AND RESULTS

As pointed out in the empirical methodology section, two econometric approaches are used: CL and NL. In Table 6.3 we show the results obtained using the CL specification. We note that the generalized Hausmann test rejects this model specification. Therefore, we concentrate our analysis and comments on the NL findings.

In Table 6.4 we show the results of our NL estimation. First of all, it is important to highlight that the Lagrange multiplier (LM) test, in both Model (1) and Model (2), rejects the null hypothesis that the inclusive values for categories (t, e) are equal to 1. As pointed out in the empirical methodology section, this implies that CL and NL give rise to different probability estimates. Further, note that the results displayed in the table include year as well as country dummies in the estimation.

We start with the description of the regression results for Model (1) where the nested structure of the two-stage decision process is the one shown in Figure 6.1. In the second column of the table we show the regression results for the *transfers decision* (first stage). In the third column we display our findings for the *effort decision* (second stage). The outcome of the empirical analysis allows us to evaluate whether and to what extent an individual's autonomy freedom and her perception of the degree of income mobility affect the probability that she chooses the combination high transfers and low effort.

As far as the effect of our primary independent variables is concerned, we can say from the outset that the theoretical model fits the data very well. Autonomy freedom determines both transfer and effort decisions as predicted by the theory. The greater the individual's level of autonomy freedom, the lower the probability that she chooses high income transfers in the first stage and the higher her optimal level of effort in the second stage. The effect of autonomy

Table 6.3. *Conditional Logit Estimation*

	Model (a) High Effort	Model (b) Low Effort
Autonomy Freedom	0.066***	−0.097***
	(0.005)	(0.023)
Gender	0.199***	−0.043
	(0.023)	(0.108)
Age	−0.002**	0.041***
	(0.001)	(0.004)
Income Mobility (ϑ)	−0.206***	0.274**
	(0.025)	(0.124)
Education	0.307***	−0.390***
	(0.017)	(0.089)
Single	−0.101**	0.691***
	(0.041)	(0.153)
Married	0.141***	−0.417***
	(0.032)	(0.123)
Religiosity	−0.156***	0.215***
	(0.013)	(0.059)
Health Status	−0.101***	0.231***
	(0.014)	(0.060)
Dummies Country	YES	YES
Dummies Time	YES	YES
Weights	YES	YES
Log-Likelihood	−49,991.391	−48,232.332
Likelihood Ratio Test	12,112.835	143,210.348
	[0.000]	[0.000]
Hausman Test	11,607.16	119.15
	[0.000]	[0.000]
Number of Observations	224,370	210,200

Notes: ***, **, and * indicate significance at 10%, 5%, and 1% level, respectively. (...) denotes robust standard errors. Hausman test–null hypothesis: conditional logit is the correct specification. [...] denotes p-values.
Source: World Values Survey (2009).

freedom, therefore, is statistically significant and consistent across the two stages of the model. Thus Proposition 6.1 is confirmed by the data.

The degree of income mobility as perceived by the individual determines both the transfer and effort decisions as predicted in the

Table 6.4. *Nested Logit Estimation (first step: transfers decision: second step: effort decision)*

	Model (1)		Model (2)	
	1st Stage	**2nd Stage**	**1st Stage**	**2nd Stage**
	High Transfer	**Low Effort**	**Low Transfer**	**High Effort**
Autonomy	−0.138***	0.010***	0.040***	0.029***
Freedom	(0.040)	(0.004)	(0.012)	(0.005)
Gender	−0.071	0.003	−0.121**	0.104***
	(0.108)	(0.022)	(0.051)	(0.026)
Age	0.007*	−0.002	−0.011***	0.007***
	(0.004)	(0.003)	(0.002)	(0.001)
Income Mobility	1.325*	0.341***	−0.129**	−0.212***
(ϑ)	(0.738)	(0.092)	(0.060)	(0.032)
Education		−0.065		0.131***
		(0.068)		(0.013)
Single		−0.017		0.034
		(0.022)		(0.025)
Married		−0.011		0.036*
		(0.016)		(0.020)
Religiosity		0.002		−0.012
		(0.008)		(0.009)
Health Status		0.012		−0.028***
		(0.017)		(0.009)
Trust	−0.183***		0.173***	
	(0.035)		(0.035)	
Distance from	0.010		0.192*	
Median Income	(0.067)		(0.106)	
Self-reported	−0.095		−0.101	
Income	(0.066)		(0.107)	
Paid-Employee	−0.067**		0.073**	
	(0.034)		(0.033)	
Self-Employed	−0.213***		0.205***	
	(0.056)		(0.055)	
Political	−0.134***		0.133***	
Orientation	(0.007)		(0.007)	
Transition	1.130***		−2.935***	
Countries	(0.131)		(0.294)	
Log-Likelihood		−23,149.810		−25,808.685
Likelihood		17,863.526		11,526.804
Ratio Test		[0.000]		[0.000]

	Model (1)		Model (2)	
	1st Stage	**2nd Stage**	**1st Stage**	**2nd Stage**
	High Transfer	**Low Effort**	**Low Transfer**	**High Effort**
LM Test for Inclusive Parameters		1,201.660 [0.000]		182.687 [0.000]
Number of observations		137,220		137,220

Notes: ***, ***, and * indicate significance at 10%, 5%, and 1% level, respectively. (...) denotes robust standard errors. [...] denotes p-values.
Source: World Values Survey (2009).

theoretical model. The lower the perceived degree of income mobility, the higher the probability that the individual chooses a high level of transfers in the first stage and a low level of effort in the second stage. Again, the effect of the individual's perception of the degree of income mobility is statistically significant and consistent across the two stages of the model. Proposition 6.2, therefore, is also empirically confirmed.

Regarding the other independent variables and controls, we note that the individual's preferences for high transfers increase if the respondent is old, if she trusts others, if she is neither a paid employee nor self-employed (i.e., she is unemployed), if she is left-wing politically oriented, and if she lives in a transition country. Further, we observe that none of the control variables for the low levels of work effort are statistically significant.

Let us now move on to the estimation of Model (2). Regression results for transfer and effort decisions are shown in the fourth and fifth columns of Table 6.4. In this model we evaluate whether and to what extent, in the two-stage decision process described by Figures 6.1 and 6.2, an individual's level of autonomy freedom and her perception of the degree of income mobility in society affect the probability that she chooses the combination low transfers and high effort. As before, in the fourth column we show the estimates concerning the determinants of the *transfers decision* (first stage). In the fifth column we show the regression results related to the determinants of the *effort decision* (second stage). Again, country and year dummies are included in the estimation.

The effect of the primary independent variables is in line with the predictions of our theoretical model. This implies that the estimates shown in the fourth column of Table 6.4 are specular to those appearing in the second column of the same table. Autonomy freedom determines both transfer and effort decisions as anticipated by the theory. The greater the individual's level of autonomy freedom, the higher the probability that she chooses low income transfers in the first stage and the higher her optimal level of effort in the second stage. The effect of autonomy freedom is statistically significant and consistent across the two stages of the model. Therefore, Proposition 6.1 is once more confirmed by the data.

The degree of income mobility perceived by the individual determines both the transfer and effort decisions as predicted in the theoretical model. The higher the perceived degree of income mobility, the higher the probability that the individual chooses a low level of transfer in the first stage and a high level of effort in the second stage. Again, the effect of the individual's perception of the degree of income mobility is statistically significant and consistent across the two stages of the model. Proposition 6.2 is therefore empirically confirmed once more.

Regarding the other independent variables and controls, we note that the individual's preferences for low transfers increase if she is young and female, if she does not trust others in society, if her self-reported income is higher than the median income, if she is either a paid employee or self-employed (i.e., if she is employed), if she is right-wing politically oriented, and if she does not live in transition countries. Further, we observe that individuals are more likely to unfold higher levels of work effort if male, old, more educated, married, and in good health.

To sum up, the main result of the empirical analysis shows that high autonomous individuals not only ask for lower levels of income transfer, but are also willing to work and produce more. Differently, low autonomous individuals, ask for higher transfers and are likely to work less. Therefore, whereas in the first case high autonomous individuals are more likely to generate a productive society, in the second case low autonomous individuals are more likely to generate a rent-seeking society. Furthermore, the support of low transfers by an autonomous individual emerges out of a sense of procedural fairness whereby she believes that her economic conditions are deserved, no matter whether she is rich or poor.[1]

Robustness Check

In order to corroborate the results that support our theory, we carry out a new set of estimations. We select a different variable to proxy the individual's preferences for income transfers by considering the respondents' answers to the following WVS question (*E037 – Government responsibility*):

How would you place your views on this scale: 1 means you agree completely with the statement *people should take more responsibility to provide for themselves*; 10 means you agree completely with the statement *the government should take more responsibility to ensure that everyone is provided for*; or you can choose any number in between.

Respondents were facing a ten-point scale in which the two extremes, 1 and 10, are those defined in the preceding question. From the construction of the question, each individual's taste for income transfer is ordered in a descending fashion: High values indicate high preferences for transfers and vice versa.

---

[1] It could be argued that the concept of voters' ignorance can be used to explain our results in light of the paradox of redistribution discussed in Chapter 5. Let us consider a voter's budget set as made up of two components: income from the voter's initial endowment and income from her productive activities. Even though the former is given once and for all, the latter changes according to the available productive inputs. Autonomy freedom could be considered an element of these inputs for its effect on the individuals' commitment and hard work. Since voters may be ill-informed, the extent of autonomy freedom perceived by individuals (i.e., the extent to which individuals may increase their budget set because of productive activities) might be determined by political campaigning. This would imply that the effect an individual's level of autonomy freedom has on her preference for redistribution should be indirectly caused by electoral campaigning. This interpretation, however, does not seem to be convincing in the light of a close examination of our results. A voter's level of education and political orientation is expected to be connected to the extent to which parties and candidates affect his/her electoral preferences. Therefore, by controlling for these two characteristics of each individual, we take into account the possible effects of electoral campaigning on the voter's ignorance. The empirical results indicate that no matter the level of education and the political orientation of the individual, the higher the degree of autonomy freedom she perceives, the lower her preferences for redistribution.

Table 6.5. *Conditional Logit Estimation – Robustness Check*

	Model (c) High Effort	Model (d) Low Effort
Autonomy Freedom	0.052***	−0.080***
	(0.006)	(0.020)
Gender	0.210***	−0.035
	(0.026)	(0.104)
Age	−0.005***	0.036***
	(0.001)	(0.004)
Income Mobility (ϑ)	−0.358***	0.325***
	(0.028)	(0.122)
Education	0.150***	−0.334***
	(0.018)	(0.079)
Single	−0.115**	0.744***
	(0.046)	(0.167)
Married	0.147***	−0.370***
	(0.036)	(0.121)
Religiosity	−0.128***	0.218***
	(0.015)	(0.052)
Health Status	−0.094***	0.254***
	(0.016)	(0.057)
Log-Likelihood	−49,823.973	−48,093.854
Likelihood Ratio Test	4,813.891	10,644.890
	[0.000]	[0.000]
Hausman Test	12,324.09	168.01
	[0.000]	[0.000]
Number of Observations	224,215	210,185

Notes: ***, **, and * indicate significance at 10%, 5%, and 1% level, respectively. (...) indicates robust standard errors. Hausman test – null hypothesis: conditional logit is the correct specification. [...] denotes p-values.
Source: World Values Survey (2009).

In Table 6.5 we report the empirical estimates of the CL specification. Again, we observe that the generalized Hausman test rejects the use of this model specification. Therefore, we turn to the NL estimation whose results are reported in Table 6.6.

In Model (1a) the nested structure of the two-stage decision process focuses on the choice combination high transfer and low effort (Figure 6.1). Once more, the theoretical model fits very well the data. The greater the individual's level of autonomy freedom, the lower the probability that she chooses high income transfers in the first stage and the higher her optimal level of effort in the second stage. Furthermore, the lower the perceived degree of income mobility, the higher the probability that the individual chooses a high level of transfers in the first stage and a low level of effort in the second stage.

As far as the estimation of Model (2a) is concerned, regression results for transfer and effort decisions are shown in the fourth and fifth columns of Table 6.6. The choice combination in the two-stage decision process in this case is low transfer and high effort (see Figure 6.2). The greater the individual's level of autonomy freedom, the higher the probability that she chooses low income transfers in the first stage, and the higher her optimal level of effort in the second stage. The higher the perceived degree of income mobility, the higher the probability that the individual chooses a low level of transfer in the first stage and a high level of effort in the second stage.

Regression results displayed in Table 6.6 confirm Propositions 6.1 and 6.2 of our theoretical model and therefore can be seen as a valid robustness check for the empirical findings shown in Table 6.4.

6.6 CONCLUDING REMARKS AND POLICY IMPLICATIONS

In this chapter we argued that individual control over the determinants of income distribution, either through the working of a meritocratic society or through the functioning of an extensive welfare state, inspires fairness considerations about inequality. We pointed out that such a control is voluntarily exercised by an individual when she makes autonomous choices over the way her life turns out. The greater the exercise of a person's autonomous behavior, the more the individual is in the position to affect the level of her income and the less her support for redistribution.

The implications of our study are important with regard to the classical problem of the trade-off between freedom and income inequality in liberal democracies. The political debate over income inequality has been traditionally characterized by two opposing views. On the one hand, liberals consider economic inequality unjust and socially destructive. On the other, conservatives believe that riches are the best way to reward those who contribute the most to prosperity or

Table 6.6. *Nested Logit Estimation – Robustness Check (first step: transfers decision: second step: effort decision)*

	Model (1a)		Model (2a)	
	1st Stage	2nd Stage	1st Stage	2nd Stage
	High Transfer	Low Effort	Low Transfer	High Effort
Autonomy Freedom	−0.059*** (0.007)	0.006** (0.003)	0.057*** (0.007)	0.036*** (0.008)
Gender	−0.056* (0.032)	0.049*** (0.018)	0.045 (0.035)	0.370*** (0.042)
Age	0.001 (0.001)	−0.007*** (0.001)	−0.003*** (0.001)	−0.007*** (0.002)
Income Mobility (ϑ)	0.379*** (0.035)	0.039** (0.018)	−0.397*** (0.031)	−0.086** (0.040)
Education		0.027** (0.012)		0.063* (0.032)
Single		−0.144*** (0.031)		0.047 (0.066)
Married		0.051*** (0.019)		0.274*** (0.051)
Religiosity		−0.079*** (0.012)		−0.324*** (0.027)
Health Status		−0.068*** (0.010)		−0.067*** (0.023)
Trust	0.083** (0.036)		−0.087** (0.035)	
Distance from Median Income	−0.043 (0.033)		0.122*** (0.025)	
Self-reported Income	−0.027 (0.033)		−0.051** (0.024)	
Paid-Employee	0.011 (0.035)		0.002 (0.033)	
Self-Employed	−0.049 (0.056)		0.062 (0.053)	
Political Orientation	−0.095*** (0.007)		0.094*** (0.006)	
Transition Countries	0.792*** (0.103)		−0.619*** (0.148)	
Log-Likelihood		−25,015.643		−20,302.867

	Model (1a)		Model (2a)	
	1st Stage	2nd Stage	1st Stage	2nd Stage
	High Transfer	Low Effort	Low Transfer	High Effort
Likelihood Ratio Test	18,420.814 [0.000]		27,729.382 [0.000]	
LM Test for Inclusive Parameters	5,685.663 [0.000]		2,881.266 [0.000]	
Number of Observations	137,270		137,270	

Notes: ***, **, and * indicate significance at 10%, 5%, and 1% level, respectively. (...) indicates robust standard errors. [...] denotes p-values.
Source: World Values Survey (2009).

that a generous welfare state encourages idleness and folly among the poor. These two apparently divergent views may be reconciled in the light of the results obtained in this study. In fact, income inequality can be considered as a fair outcome according to the extent of autonomy freedom people enjoy.

For the sake of clarity, let us make an example. Consider two societies, Meritland and Luckyland, both sharing the same income distribution. However, in Meritland there is a widespread belief that economic success is dependent on effort. In this society, therefore, those born in families at the bottom of the income distribution believe that they are as likely as those born to rich parents to end up at the bottom or at the top, as do children born to well-off families. In contrast, in Luckyland people believe that effort does not pay since an individual's economic success is largely determined by environmental factors such as luck or privilege. Those born in poor families believe that they have little chance to improve their future economic conditions.

It is easy to notice that these two societies, although equally unequal in terms of income distribution, differ in the perceptions regarding the nature and causes of their inequality. Unlike people in Luckyland, those who live in Meritland consider income dynamics fair since effort, skills, and commitment are justly rewarded. Individuals in Meritland are, therefore, likely to be more tolerant of existing inequalities in the distribution of income than those living in Luckyland. The fact that these two societies are polar cases facilitates our understanding of the importance that people's attitudes toward inequality have on their preferences for redistribution. In Meritland, the widespread belief of living in a just world in which the process of social mobility is driven by effort would lead to a demand for low levels of income redistribution. On the contrary, in Luckyland the view that income dynamics is unjust because it is based on luck and privilege leads individuals to demand large redistributive schemes.

Summarizing the main message of the example, we can say that individuals consider income inequality fair if the pretax distribution of income is perceived to be caused by factors under their volitional control such as effort, and they consider the pre-tax distribution of income unfair if it is perceived as caused by circumstances beyond individual control such as luck or privilege. The individual's control over the determinants of income distribution, either through the working of a meritocratic society or through the functioning of an extensive welfare state seems, therefore, to inspire fairness considerations about income inequality.

In this context, however, one important question still remains unanswered: When are individuals in the position to affect and, therefore, control the pretax distribution of income? In this chapter we argued that the development of a person's autonomy freedom is closely connected with her ability to make choices that express volitional control over the way her life turns out. The fuller the exercise of a person's autonomous behavior, the more the individual is in the position to affect the pretax distribution of income and the less her support for redistribution. On the contrary, in societies where individuals are not autonomous and do not determine the sources of their incomes, state intervention via redistribution schemes is instrumental in order to guarantee social justice.

These findings are better understood if social mobility is interpreted in procedural terms. It is not the degree of inequality that matters but the process that brought it about. Two different societies may, therefore, present the same income inequality, but they can differ in fairness according to the extent of autonomy freedom people enjoy in each of them.

The results obtained in this chapter on the relationship between autonomy freedom and preferences for redistribution may be also interpreted in light of the political culture theory (Inglehart and Welzel, 2005). In this branch of research, societies can be grouped according to their respective cultural ways of life. According to Douglas and Wildavsky (1983), societies can be distinguished as egalitarian/collectivistic or hierarchical/individualistic. The former exhibit high degrees of collective control and egalitarian ordering, whereas the latter are characterized by greater emphasis on authority and individual self-sufficiency. Egalitarian/collectivistic societies can be expected to be populated by less autonomous individuals whose preferences for redistribution are more likely driven by a notion of distributive justice that focuses on outcomes rather than processes. On the contrary, hierarchical/individualistic societies can be considered as those in which individuals are more autonomous and whose preferences for redistribution are more likely guided by a notion of distributive justice based on processes rather than outcomes.

7

Autonomy Freedom and Welfare Spending

7.1 INTRODUCTION

In Chapter 6 we demonstrated that the level of autonomy freedom enjoyed by individuals affects their attitudes toward inequality and, therefore, shapes their preferences for redistribution. More specifically, we argued that individuals form their tastes for income transfers out of a principle of procedural fairness based on the extent of autonomy freedom they possess. The higher an individual's level of autonomy freedom, the stronger her belief to be in control of her actions and their consequences, and the more accountable she feels as far as her income level is concerned. It follows that, whatever her economic status, she thinks that it is deserved. Therefore, for a highly autonomous individual, transfers are not just, even if to her benefit. The opposite applies for nonautonomous individuals. The lower an individual's level of autonomy freedom, the less she feels in control of her actions and their consequences, and the less accountable she is as far as her income level is concerned. Therefore, whatever her economic status, she thinks that it is not deserved. In this perspective, to a nonautonomous individual, transfers are necessary to compensate for unfairness in the income generation process.

In the present chapter we move from an analysis exclusively focussed on individual preferences for redistribution and income transfers to another that looks also at the determinants of actual social expenditure. Therefore, the objective of this chapter is to examine the relationship between autonomy freedom, individual preference for redistribution, and actual welfare spending.

Social welfare spending is probably the major fiscal policy instrument in the government's hands to fight inequality. Several measures are constructed to calculate the extent of income inequality. Among them, the most frequently used is the Gini coefficient. Such a measure is largely adopted to evaluate the effectiveness of state interventions to reduce unequal distribution of incomes and poverty. Our first concern is to examine whether actual inequality – measured by the Gini coefficient – explains welfare spending in OECD countries. In this respect, we survey a dominant strand of the literature that suggests that countries characterized by greater pretax and transfer income inequality are those that display lower levels of social expenditure. This result offers the basis for arguing that it is not actual inequality that affects government decisions regarding the size of the welfare state, but the attitudes that voters have toward inequality and redistribution.

Since in democratic systems citizens vote and elect their government, their perceptions and preferences are expected to influence policy choices. If we believe that governments ought to be responsive to the wishes of the electorate, redistributive policies should be largely driven by the preferences that individuals have about inequality and redistribution. If this is the case, since people's tastes for income transfers are significantly affected by the level of autonomy freedom individuals enjoy (Chapter 6), we should expect that autonomy freedom determines also the extent of welfare spending. In this chapter, we test these hypotheses using data from the OECD countries and find support to our predictions.

7.2 INCOME INEQUALITY AND WELFARE SPENDING

Levels and Trends in the OECD Countries

We start with the analysis of the levels of income inequality across the OECD countries. The measure of inequality that we use to make the cross-country comparisons is the standard Gini coefficient. It ranges from 0, which indicates perfect equality in the distribution of income, to 100, which indicates perfect inequality. According to this measure, perfect equality is achieved when each share of the population gets the same share of the total income. On the contrary, perfect inequality is reached when total income goes to the share of the population with the highest income.[1]

In Table 7.1 we report the Gini coefficients for the OECD countries over a time span that goes from 1980 to 2005. We note that inequality varies between a minimum level (19.75) in Sweden in the 1980s to a maximum level (51.86) in Mexico in the 1990s. We also note that, according to their respective Gini coefficients, countries can be generally grouped into four categories:

1. Countries with income inequality always below the OECD average: Sweden, Finland, Denmark, Norway, Austria, Luxembourg, New Zealand, Czech Republic, Germany, Netherlands, Belgium, Iceland, Switzerland, and Slovakia;
2. Countries with income inequality around the OECD average: Canada, Australia, France, Hungary, and Korea;
3. Countries with inequality in income always greater than the OECD average: Japan, Italy, Spain, United Kingdom, Ireland, Greece, Portugal, United States, and Poland;
4. Outlier countries with income inequality significantly higher than the OECD average: Turkey and Mexico.

In Table 7.2 we summarize the changes in income inequality levels based on variations of the Gini coefficients over time. We focus on two time periods: 1980s to 1990s and 1990s to 2005.

We observe a common trend in the first period with more than a half of the OECD countries (fourteen out of twenty-four) experiencing a rise in the Gini coefficient (i.e., an increase in the level of income inequality). In seven countries inequality remains stable, and in only three does it decline. Unlike the first time interval, in the second time period (1990 to 2005) a common trend does not seem to emerge. In eleven countries inequality increases, in eight countries it is stable, and in six it declines. However, it is interesting to note that Finland, Sweden, Norway, Germany, and the United States are countries that, during the

---

[1] The Gini coefficient measures the extent to which the distribution of income among individuals deviates from a perfectly equal distribution. A Lorenz curve plots the cumulative percentage of total income received against the cumulative proportion of recipients, starting with the poorest individual. The Gini coefficient ranges between 0 (perfect equality) and 100 (perfect inequality) and is calculated as follows: $\frac{1}{2n^2\bar{y}} \sum_{i=1}^{n} \sum_{j=1}^{n} |y_i - y_j|$.

Table 7.1. *Levels of Gini Coefficients: OECD countries, 1980–2005*

Country	Years		
	1980s	**1990s**	**2000–05**
Australia	na	30.91	30.11
Austria	23.60	23.80	26.53
Belgium	27.37	28.65	27.10
Canada	28.69	28.28	31.69
Czech Republic	25.73	25.73	26.80
Denmark	22.09	21.49	23.24
Finland	20.67	22.79	26.91
France	30.00	27.00	27.00
Germany	25.75	27.22	29.81
Greece	33.58	33.56	32.08
Hungary	29.35	29.35	29.07
Iceland	na	na	27.96
Ireland	33.06	32.43	32.84
Italy	30.88	34.79	35.19
Japan	30.45	32.35	32.05
Korea	na	na	31.24
Luxembourg	24.71	25.90	25.80
Mexico	45.23	51.86	47.36
Netherlands	25.90	28.25	27.12
New Zealand	27.10	33.50	33.50
Norway	23.40	25.60	27.60
Poland	na	na	37.21
Portugal	35.92	35.92	38.46
Slovakia	na	na	26.80
Spain	37.08	34.29	31.87
Sweden	19.75	21.13	23.41
Switzerland	na	na	27.56
Turkey	43.42	49.00	43.00
United Kingdom	32.53	35.40	33.50
United States	33.75	36.14	38.14
OECD	29.6	31.0	31.0

Source: OECD Social Indicators database.

two time periods under consideration, do not experience changes in inequality trends. In these countries, inequality keeps rising over time. On the other hand, Spain is the only country in which income inequality shows a continuous decline during the period 1980–2005.

Table 7.2. *Trends in Income Inequality: OECD Countries, 1980–2005*

Time Period	Inequality Trends		
	Decline	**No Change**	**Increase**
1980s to 1990s	Czech Rep.	Austria	Belgium
	France	Canada	Finland
	Spain	Denmark	Germany
		Greece	Italy
		Hungary	Japan
		Ireland	Luxembourg
		Portugal	Mexico
			Netherlands
			New Zealand
			Norway
			Sweden
			Turkey
			United Kingdom
			United States
1990s to 2005	Belgium	Australia	Austria
	Mexico	France	Canada
	Netherlands	Hungary	Denmark
	Spain	Ireland	Finland
	Turkey	Italy	Germany
	United Kingdom	Japan	Greece
		Luxembourg	Norway
		New Zealand	Portugal
			Sweden
			United States

Source: OECD Social Indicators database.

Fighting inequality is one of the major task of governments. Social expenditure as a percentage of GDP can be seen as a measure of the extent to which governments assume responsibility for reducing income inequality and supporting the standard of living of the poor. Social expenditure comprises both in-kind provision of goods and services and financial support through cash benefits and tax advantages. For cross-country comparisons, the most commonly used indicator of social expenditure is public spending as a share of GDP. Social expenditures are classified as public when general government (i.e., central administration, local governments, and social security institutions) controls the relevant financial flows (OECD, 2006).

Table 7.3. *Public Social Expenditure as a Share of GDP: OECD Countries, 1980–2005*

Country	1980	1985	1990	1995	2000	2005	Average 1980–2005
Australia	11.3	13.5	14.2	17.8	18.6	17.1	15.5
Austria	22.5	24.1	24.1	26.6	26.0	27.2	25.1
Belgium	24.1	26.9	26.9	28.1	26.7	26.4	26.5
Canada	14.3	17.4	18.6	19.6	17.3	16.5	17.4
Czech Republic	na	na	17.0	18.9	20.3	19.5	19.1
Denmark	29.1	27.9	29.3	32.4	28.9	27.1	29.1
Finland	18.5	23.0	24.8	31.1	24.5	26.1	24.5
France	21.1	26.6	26.6	29.2	28.3	29.2	26.8
Germany	23.0	23.6	22.8	27.5	27.2	26.7	25.1
Greece	11.5	17.9	20.9	21.4	23.6	20.5	19.2
Hungary	na	na	na	na	20.0	22.5	20.7
Iceland	na	na	16.4	19.0	19.7	16.9	18.0
Ireland	17.0	22.1	18.6	19.4	13.6	16.7	17.7
Italy	18.4	21.3	23.3	23.0	24.1	25.0	22.4
Japan	10.2	11.0	11.2	13.5	16.1	18.6	13.3
Korea	na	na	3.1	3.6	5.6	6.9	4.5
Luxembourg	23.5	23.0	21.9	23.8	20.0	23.2	22.4
Mexico	na	1.8	3.8	8.1	9.9	7.4	6.1
Netherlands	26.9	27.3	27.6	25.6	21.8	20.9	25.0
New Zealand	17.2	18.1	21.9	18.9	19.2	18.5	19.0
Norway	17.9	19.1	24.7	26.0	23.0	21.6	22.2
Poland	na	na	15.5	23.8	21.9	21.0	20.7
Portugal	10.9	11.1	13.9	18.0	20.5	...	16.0
Slovak Republic	na	na	na	19.2	18.3	16.6	18.2
Spain	15.9	18.2	19.5	21.4	19.9	21.2	19.3
Sweden	28.8	30.0	30.8	33.0	28.6	29.4	30.1
Switzerland	14.2	15.1	17.9	23.9	25.4	20.3	19.3
Turkey	4.3	4.2	7.6	7.5	na	13.7	7.5
United Kingdom	17.9	21.1	19.5	23.0	21.7	21.3	20.6
United States	13.3	13.0	13.4	15.5	14.2	15.9	14.2
OECD	17.9	19.1	19.1	21.3	20.2	20.6	19.6

Source: OECD Social Indicators database.

In Table 7.3 we report data on public social expenditure as a share of GDP for the OECD countries over a time period going from 1980 to 2005. The spending flows are recorded on a gross basis (i.e., before deduction of tax payments and before addition of tax expenditures provided for social purposes). Social spending is averaged at country level in the last column of the table.

We note that in the OECD countries gross social expenditure has increased from about 18 percent to 20 percent in the period 1980–2005. Although social spending dynamics in the OECD countries differ, on average social spending-to-GDP ratios increased most significantly in the beginning of both the 1980s and the 1990s. The two major determinants of the rise in social expenditure have been the increased support for the growing retired population and health spending. Projections regarding population growth indicate expected further increases in these two important areas of social expenditure in the future.

As far as the level of social expenditure in percentage of GDP is concerned, we observe that it varies between a minimum of 1.8 percent in Mexico in 1985 to a maximum of 33 percent in Sweden in 1995. We also note that, according to the average level of their social spending during the twenty-five years under investigation, the OECD countries can be grouped in four categories:

1. Countries with average social expenditure below the OECD average: Australia, Canada, Czech Republic, Iceland, Ireland, Japan, Portugal, Switzerland, and United States;
2. Countries with average social expenditure around the OECD average: Greece, New Zealand, Slovak Republic, Spain, and United Kingdom;
3. Countries with average social expenditure greater than the OECD average: Austria, Belgium, Denmark, Finland, France, Germany, Hungary, Italy, Luxembourg, Netherlands, Norway, Portugal, and Sweden;
4. Outlier countries with average social expenditure significantly lower than the OECD average: Turkey and Mexico.

Total social expenditure can be disaggregated into several broad social policy areas. In Table 7.4 we show four categories of social spending as percent of GDP for the year 2005. We note that the three biggest groups of social transfers are pensions (on average about 7 percent), health (on average about 5 percent), and income transfers to the working-age population (on average about 4 percent). Public spending on other social services only exceeds 4 percent of GDP in the Nordic countries, where the public role in providing services to the elderly, the disabled, and families is the most extensive.

Table 7.4. *Public Social Expenditure as a Share of GDP by Main Social Policy Areas: OECD Countries, 2005*

Country	Pensions	Income Support to the Working Age Population	Health	All Social Services Except Health	Total Public Social Spending
Australia	4.2	5.3	5.9	1.4	17.1
Austria	12.9	6.0	5.2	1.2	27.2
Belgium	11.2	6.6	6.4	1.7	26.4
Canada	5.2	2.3	6.3	2.4	16.5
Czech Republic	7.3	4.2	6.3	0.8	19.5
Denmark	6.1	8.3	7.1	5.1	27.1
Finland	8.0	7.3	5.3	4.2	26.1
France	11.9	6.0	7.2	2.0	29.2
Germany	11.2	4.5	8.0	2.6	26.7
Greece	11.6	2.5	4.2	1.9	20.5
Hungary	7.7	5.3	5.1	1.5	22.5
Iceland	4.4	3.5	5.7	3.2	16.9
Ireland	3.2	4.4	4.9	0.6	16.7
Italy	13.8	3.3	6.3	0.6	25.0
Japan	7.6	1.5	6.3	1.3	18.6
Korea	1.3	1.0	3.2	0.3	6.9
Luxembourg	8.0	6.5	4.8	1.4	23.2
Mexico	4.1	0.4	2.2	0.6	7.4
Netherlands	6.4	6.9	5.7	1.2	20.9
New Zealand	4.9	6.7	6.1	0.3	18.5
Norway	4.6	6.3	5.8	4.5	21.6
Poland	9.3	6.6	4.2	0.6	21.0
Portugal	9.1	4.2	6.3	1.0	23.5
Slovak Republic	5.9	5.1	4.6	0.6	16.6
Spain	8.7	4.1	5.4	0.6	21.2
Sweden	9.1	6.8	7.4	5.8	29.4
Switzerland	9.3	4.5	5.2	1.2	20.3
Turkey	6.3	2.6	3.9	0.2	13.7
United Kingdom	8.3	5.6	6.1	1.2	21.3
United States	6.1	1.8	6.2	0.5	15.9
OECD	7.4	4.6	5.4	1.7	20.1

Source: OECD Social Indicators database.

Does Income Inequality Affect Welfare Spending?

The political economy model of redistribution suggests that higher inequality in the distribution of income is associated with greater levels of political support for welfare spending. This result is due to a series of seminal works by Romer (1975), Roberts (1977), and Meltzer and Richards (1981). These scholars were motivated by the empirical evidence that the distribution of income is generally skewed with small numbers of large incomes. This implies that average income is above median income. Since in simple models of democracy the voter with the median income is decisive, such a voter is expected to influence government spending. In this framework, the key variable is the ratio of the median income to the mean income. The lower such a ratio (i.e., the more skewed the distribution of income), the higher the level of welfare expenditure desired by the majority of voters. Therefore, the greater the pretax and transfer inequality in the distribution of income, the greater the electoral support for government policies that redistribute wealth from rich to poor and the higher welfare spending.

The political economy models of redistribution are intuitively compelling. For those with egalitarian sympathies, their policy implications are encouraging, as they suggest that market inequalities can be offset, to a certain extent, by redistribution.

The hypothesis of an inverse relationship between inequality and redistribution has been evaluated in a number of empirical studies. In these studies the estimated equation to test the median-voter model of redistribution takes the following form:

$$R = \alpha + \beta I + \gamma z + \varepsilon$$

where R indicates the extent of redistributive public spending, I is the degree of inequality, z is a vector of control variables, and ε is a stochastic error term. The empirical literature on the relationship between income inequality and welfare spending focused on two research questions: whether β in the relationship between income inequality and redistributive public spending is a positive and significant parameter, and whether the median voter plays a role in explaining the relationship between inequality and redistribution.

Previous attempts to validate the theoretical predictions of the political economy model of redistribution have been disappointing. Perotti (1996) finds no significant relationship between inequality and social expenditure in a sample of fifty rich and poor countries. Rodriguez (2004) shows that income inequality is associated with less, not more, social expenditure. With some notable exceptions (Persson and Tabellini, 1994; Milanovic, 2000), more recent papers show that advanced industrialized countries with a comparatively high level of pretransfer inequality spend less on welfare and redistribute less than countries with a low level of pretransfer inequality (Bradley et al., 2003; Moene and Wallerstein, 2001, 2003; Iversen and Soskice, 2006).

Since the publication of the political economy models of redistribution, their predictions about the relationship between inequality and redistribution did not fare so well when confronted with data. As mentioned previously, by and large, empirical studies have produced results in contrast with the outcome expected in the basic theoretical model. The fact that countries with larger pretax income inequality are those characterized by less generous government welfare programs has been defined as one of the relevant unsolved puzzles in modern comparative political economy (Iversen, 2005).

Despite disappointment for these results, the empirical literature on the determinants of welfare spending suggests that there are many other potential differences between countries that may affect the link between income inequality and redistribution. Societal divisions along ethnic and religious lines as well as different political systems ought to be taken into account when the relationship between unequal distribution of incomes and welfare spending is examined (Alesina and La Ferrara, 2005; Persson and Tabellini, 2000). Furthermore, other considerations highlight some theoretical limitations of the traditional political economy model of redistribution. One such limitation is the fact that the basic model neglects that voting and other political decisions may be based on a variety of issues beyond redistributive policy (Roemer, 1998; Boldrin and Montes, 2005). This may reduce the political decisiveness of voters with median income.

In Chapter 5 we dwelled upon a literature suggesting that voters' preferences for redistribution may be guided by values rather than pecuniary self-interest. Concepts such as individual's beliefs about the determinants of wealth as well as fairness concerns about inequality can be crucial factors affecting the extent of redistribution (Piketty, 1995; Bénabou and Tirole, 2006). Within this line of research, in Chapter 6 we proposed a model that links the extent of autonomy freedom enjoyed by individuals with their tastes for income transfers. More specifically, we argued that it is not the extent of inequality that affects individual preferences for redistribution, but rather the individual perceptions about the sources of inequality. We demonstrated that autonomy freedom shapes those perceptions, and in this chapter our objective is to examine whether it may indirectly affect welfare spending, too. This is the subject matter of the next section.

7.3 AUTONOMY FREEDOM AND WELFARE SPENDING

From Individual Preferences to Policy Choices

The application of the principle of procedural fairness at the individual level developed in Chapter 6 can be extended at the society level if we examine the effect of autonomy freedom on the preferences for income transfer when both variables are aggregated at the country level. This allows us to evaluate whether the principle of procedural fairness that exists at the individual level guides the redistributive preferences of the society as a whole.

In Figure 7.1 we show the correlation between autonomy freedom and preferences for redistribution both calculated at the aggregate level for the OECD countries. We observe that, as we move from countries characterized by a low extent of autonomy freedom to countries with high degrees of autonomy freedom (i.e., as we move rightward on the horizontal axis), the level of welfare spending as a percentage of GDP decreases. This preliminary descriptive result suggests that autonomy freedom affects government redistributive policies since it shapes individual preferences for redistribution.

The relationship displayed in Figure 7.1 is descriptive. It needs an appropriate evaluation by means of an econometric exercise. Thus, we test the negative effect of the aggregate level of autonomy freedom on society's preferences for income transfers by estimating the following ordinary least square (OLS) model:

$$PrfTrn_{i,t} = \alpha + \beta AF_{i,t} + \gamma K_{i,t} + \delta X_{i,t} + \lambda Z_{i,t} + \eta_i + \mu_t + \epsilon_{i,t}$$

where *PrfTrn* are society's preferences for transfers in country i in the year t, AF is the average level of autonomy freedom enjoyed by individuals in country i in the year t, K is the vector of independent variables drawn from the literature on the determinants of redistribution and welfare spending for country i in time t, X is a vector of demographic

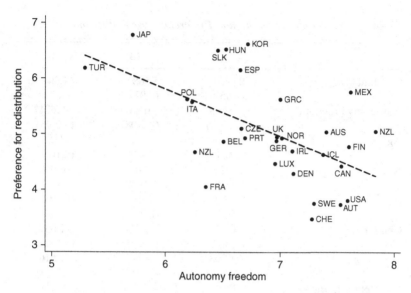

Figure 7.1. Autonomy Freedom and Preferences for Redistribution.

characteristics of country i in time t, Z is a vector of macroeconomic variables for country i in time t, ϵ is the i.i.d. error term, α, α, γ, δ and λ are the coefficients and, finally, η and μ are the country and the year dummies, respectively.

In Table 7.5 we report the empirical results. Three different models are displayed in the table – Models (a), (b) and (c). In Model (a) we estimate the effect of autonomy freedom on the individual preferences for income transfers calculated both at the country level with the inclusion of some demographic variables. We note that the effect of autonomy freedom is negative and statistically significant. This indicates that, the greater the average level of autonomy freedom in a given OECD country, the higher people's support for low transfers. The average age, gender, and self-reported income of respondents do not seem to affect in a statistically significant way individual preferences for redistribution at the country level. Unlike other demographic controls, the higher the average education of respondents, the lower their support for redistribution.

In Model (b) we estimate the effect that the level of autonomy freedom in a given OECD country has on the preferences for income transfers expressed by that society as a whole by including

Table 7.5. *Autonomy Freedom and Preferences for Redistribution*

	(a)	(b)	(c)
Constant	93.251	5.588	11.006
	(0.55)	(0.03)	(0.07)
Autonomy Freedom	−0.588***	−0.667***	−0.671***
	(−2.72)	(−3.08)	(−2.95)
Age	−5.362	1.623	1.275
	(−0.44)	(0.13)	(0.10)
Age^2	0.115	−0.058	−0.049
	−0.39	(−0.20)	(−0.17)
Age^3	−0.001	0.001	0.001
	(−0.35)	(0.24)	(0.21)
Gender	−0.742	−1.701	−1.637
	(−0.22)	(−0.45)	(−0.44)
Education	−1.203*	−1.644**	−1.616**
	(−1.80)	(−2.42)	(−2.28)
Self-Reported Income	−0.048	−0.118	−0.114
	(−0.45)	(−0.90)	(−0.84)
Trust		−2.342*	−2.342*
		(−1.67)	(−1.66)
Religiosity		0.155	0.15
		(0.24)	(0.23)
Transition Countries		0.692**	0.728*
		(2.00)	(1.76)
GDP Growth Rate			0.005
			(0.16)
Number of Observations	52	52	52
Overal Significance	78.103	112.764	109.505
	[0.000]	[0.000]	[0.000]
R^2	0.552	0.629	0.629

Notes: ***, **, and * indicate significance at 10%, 5%, and 1% level, respectively. (…) denotes robust standard errors. […] denotes p-values.
Source: World Values Survey (2009) and World Development Indicators (2009).

demographic controls as well as some independent variables drawn from the literature on the determinants of individual tastes for redistribution and the size of welfare spending. We note that the effect of autonomy freedom is still significant and negative. As far as the demographic controls are concerned, age, gender, and self-reported income are not significant, whereas education keeps its negative and significant effect on the individuals' preferences for transfers. We use trust to proxy fractionalization in society by assuming that the more people trust each others, the lower the level of fractionalization. We note that, in line with the main literature on the effect of fractionalization on individual preferences for redistribution, the more individuals trust each others, the greater their support for income transfers. The effect of religiosity on the individual preferences for redistribution displays the expected sign but does not seem to have a statistically significant effect. According to the predictions supported in the literature, individuals living in transition economies (i.e., former communist countries) show greater support for income transfers. In Model (c) we add the GDP growth rate among the regressors, which does not seem to influence significantly individual preferences for redistribution. It is important to note that all the variables used in the empirical analysis behave consistently across the three model specifications.

The econometric results reported in Table 7.5 support at the aggregate level the effect of autonomy freedom on the individual preferences for income transfers. This implies that the principle of procedural fairness discussed in Chapter 6 operates at both the individual and the country level. Therefore, the greater the autonomy freedom individuals enjoy, the more they believe that the actual distribution of income is just, and the lower their support for redistribution. On the other hand, the lower the autonomy freedom individuals enjoy, the more they believe that the actual distribution of income is unjust, and the higher their support for redistribution.

The fact that the country level of autonomy freedom affects the perceptions about inequality shared by individuals in society leads to a negative, albeit indirect, relationship between the extent of autonomy freedom and government redistributive policies. In countries characterized by low levels of autonomy freedom, individuals do not determine the sources of their incomes and, therefore, demand state intervention via redistribution to guarantee social justice. In these countries, governments are keen to fulfill their voters' desire and are expected to implement large redistributive plans. Differently, in countries with high autonomy freedom, individuals perceive income distribution as fair, and social justice is guaranteed by the control that people exercise over the way their lives turn out. In the latter countries, in order to reduce inequality, the role of government is limited and, as a consequence, welfare spending is expected to be lower.

Autonomy Freedom and Welfare Spending: A Taxonomy of
Welfare Systems

In Figure 7.2 we display the relationship between autonomy freedom
and welfare spending on a four quadrant diagram. Both variables are
collected for the OECD countries and are averaged at country level.
A visual inspection of the figure reveals that each country is located in
one of the four quadrants according to the combination between the
extent of autonomy freedom and the level of social expenditure.

We observe that countries located in the North–West/South–East
diagonal display combinations of autonomy freedom and welfare
spending consistent with the principle of procedural fairness that,
according to our findings, inspires individual preferences for redistribution. More specifically, in the North–West quadrant we find countries
that display low degrees of autonomy freedom and high levels of
welfare spending. This combination of the two variables in the axes
characterizes countries whose welfare system is designed on the basis
of traditional social democratic political attitudes. In the South–East
quadrant, we find countries that display high degrees of autonomy

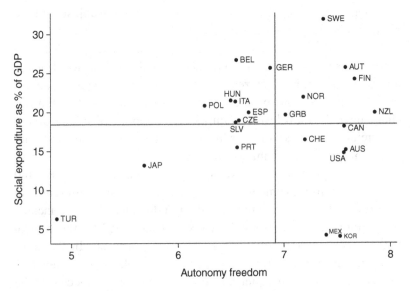

Figure 7.2. Taxonomy of Welfare Systems.

freedom and low levels of welfare spending. These countries are characterized by a combination of free market liberalism and a widely shared view that individuals can work by themselves the way to success in a society that, by design, rewards merit and hard work and punishes idleness and lack of effort.

The OECD countries located in the South–West/North–East diagonal display a combination of autonomy freedom and welfare spending not consistent with the analysis developed in Chapter 6. The relationship between autonomy freedom and welfare spending is no longer negative. The data actually indicate that a high level of autonomy freedom is correlated with a high social expenditure as percentage of GDP. In the South–West quadrant lie countries that show low levels of both autonomy freedom and welfare spending. Most of these countries are transition economies with welfare systems that are evolving over time. In this quadrant the only exceptions are Turkey and Japan namely countries where we expect to observe thicker social ties and comparatively rigid hierarchical structures. In these societies the combination of low autonomy freedom and limited welfare spending might be justified in light of the protection that social, religious, and political communities provide to their members. In the North–East quadrant, we find countries that show high degrees of autonomy freedom and high levels of welfare transfers. These are the modern social democracies where social justice is associated with economic policies that support merit, equality of opportunity, and competition. Such a philosophy of government rejects both socialism and laissez-faire approaches and chiefly stresses education and competitive mechanisms to pursue economic progress.

How do we square the position of the last two sets of countries in Figure 7.2 with our interpretation of procedural fairness? The most immediate answer is to consider the countries located along the South–West/North–East diagonal as those in which the principle of procedural fairness to shape individual preferences for inequality and redistribution does not apply. However, such an interpretation is too simplistic since it is based on a diagram that merely show differences from the means in the values of the two variables under observation.

A more accurate analysis is required to understand the intuition behind what is shown in Figure 7.2. To this end, we carry out a sensitivity analysis to test the robustness of the negative relationship between autonomy freedom and welfare spending in the OECD countries under investigation. We then estimate the following equation:

$$WSp_{i,t} = \alpha_{i,t} + \beta AF_{i,t} + \gamma z + \epsilon_{i,t}$$

where WSp is the level of welfare spending as percentage of GDP of country i at time t, AF indicate country i's level of autonomy freedom in time t, z indicates a vector of control variables, and ϵ is the i.i.d. error term. The superscript s indicates that in carrying out the empirical analysis we consider all the OECD countries (in which case $s =$ all OECD countries) as well as different subsamples in which single OECD countries are one by one removed from the analysis to test the robustness of the regression results (in which case $s =$ all OECD countries but one, all OECD countries but two, etc.).

In Table 7.6 we display the econometric results of our sensitivity analysis. For the sake of simplicity, we start with running a simplified version of the preceding estimated equation in which controls are not taken into account. We show several model specifications according to the number of OECD countries considered in the analysis. In Model (a) we take into consideration all the OECD countries. We note that the relationship between autonomy freedom and social expenditure displays the wrong sign and, more importantly, is not statistically significant. This result seems to indicate that autonomy freedom does not affect welfare spending in OECD countries. This would imply that the principle of procedural fairness does not affect government's redistributive policy choices.

In the next two models, we run the regression after removing from the set of countries Turkey in Model (b) and Japan in Model (c). The choice to remove these two countries is determined by the fact that, by looking at Figure 7.2, they are located at the greatest distance from the North–West/South–East diagonal. Results indicate that, although the signs of the autonomy freedom coefficients are correct, the relationship between autonomy freedom and welfare spending is still not statistically significant. Again, the principle of procedural fairness does not seem to determine welfare spending by affecting the individual tastes for redistribution.

However, if we implement the estimation by removing both Turkey and Japan from our set of OECD countries (see Model (d)), we find that the relationship between autonomy freedom and welfare spending

Table 7.6. *Autonomy Freedom and Welfare Spending: Sensitivity Analysis*

	(a)	(b)	(c)	(d)	(e)	(f)
Constant	14.610	26.947***	20.160	39.682***	40.940***	47.401***
	(10.125)	(10.206)	(12.403)	(10.042)	(9.896)	(9.718)
Autonomy Freedom	0.621	−1.103	−0.142	−2.861*	−3.081**	−4.073***
	(1.483)	(1.492)	(1.785)	(1.469)	(1.445)	(1.416)
Log-Likelihood	−182.93	−173.94	−173.56	−162.82	−157.14	−146.03
Number of Observations	56	54	53	51	50	47
Overall Significance	0.176	0.546	0.006	3.795	4.549	8.271
	[0.452]	[0.645]	[0.932]	[0.004]	[0.000]	[0.000]
R^2	0.005	0.012	0.000	0.068	0.087	0.149

Notes: Model (a): OECD countries; Model (b): OECD without Turkey; Model (c): OECD without Japan; Model (d): OECD without Turkey and Japan; Model (e): OECD without Turkey, Japan, and Sweden; Model (f): OECD Without Turkey, Japan, Sweden, and Finland. ***, **, and * indicate significance at 10%, 5%, and 1% level, respectively. (…) denotes robust standard errors. [...] denotes p-values.

Source: World Values Survey (2009) and OECD Social Indicators Database (2009).

is negative and statistically significant, as we would expect. The principle of procedural fairness now operates successfully to affect welfare expenditure of the OECD countries by shaping individual preferences toward inequality and redistribution. It is important to note that if we keep removing countries on the basis of their distance from the mean values of autonomy freedom and welfare spending, the quality of the regression increases. In Model (e) we add Sweden to the list of removed countries and in Model (f), Finland. We note that as we move from Model (d) to Model (f), autonomy freedom remains statistically significant, and the fit of the regression improves across the different model specifications.

The empirical estimates in Table 7.6 coupled with the results shown in Figure 7.2 demonstrate that, with the exception of Turkey and Japan social public expenditure is influenced by the level of autonomy freedom existing in the OECD countries. More specifically, in these countries, though to a different degree, government welfare policies correct unjust distortions in the process that determines the economic successes or failures of people in society. These distortions depend on the extent of autonomy freedom individuals enjoy. The higher autonomy freedom, the fairer, in procedural terms, the process that affects economic successes or failures, and the less welfare spending.

To check for the robustness of the results obtained in Table 7.6, we reestimate the model specification (d) with the inclusion of other independent variables chosen on the basis of the determinants of welfare spending suggested in the economic literature (Chapter 5). The regression estimates are shown in Table 7.7. They indicate that, according to the principle of procedural fairness, countries characterized by higher levels of autonomy freedom spend less in welfare and vice versa. As we move from model specification (a) to (b) and to (c), the statistical significance of the effect of autonomy freedom increases with the inclusion of further independent variables in the estimated equation. We also note that higher levels of trust are associated with lower welfare spending. We interpret this result as a further confirmation of the finding of Alesina and La Ferrara (2005): Highly fractionalized societies are more likely to oppose redistribution. As expected, welfare spending increases as the age of the population and the GDP percapita rise. Finally, the degree of market openness does not seem

Table 7.7. *Autonomy Freedom and Welfare Spending*

	(a)	(b)	(c)
Constant	39.682***	26.776	29.126
	(10.042)	(20.181)	(20.497)
Autonomy Freedom	−2.861*	−2.643**	−4.060***
	(1.469)	(1.263)	(1.303)
Trust		−16.569***	−10.035*
		(5.069)	(6.062)
Age		0.829***	0.685**
		(0.290)	(0.270)
Openness		0.023	0.012
		(0.019)	(0.016)
GDP per Capita			0.000***
			(0.000)
Log-Likelihood	−162.82	−153.56	−149.98
Number of Observations	51	51	51
Overal Significance	3.795	8.592	10.353
	[0.002]	[0.000]	[0.000]
R^2	0.068	0.352	0.437

Notes: ***, **, and * denote significance at 10%, 5%, and 1% level, respectively. (...) denotes robust standard errors. [...] denotes p-values.
Source: World Values Survey (2009), World Development Indicators (2009), and OECD Social Indicators Database (2009)

to have a statistically significant impact on social expenditure in the OECD countries.

7.4 CONCLUDING REMARKS

In this chapter our aim was to demonstrate that the level of autonomy freedom enjoyed by individuals is also an important determinant of welfare spending in the OECD countries. We showed that, when aggregated at the country level, autonomy freedom affects people's attitudes toward inequality and the preferences for redistribution of the society as a whole. This effect brings about the indirect result of influencing government redistributive policies. The greater the extent of autonomy freedom enjoyed by the population in a given country, the greater people's demand for low levels of redistribution, and the smaller the size of welfare spending. Underneath this chain of causes and effects a principle of procedural fairness lies that operates at the individual level as well as at the country level. In this context, redistributive policies are not aimed at reducing income inequality per se, but their goal is to correct unjust mechanisms that determine either economic successes or failures in people's life. Countries in which individuals believe that effort and merit are rewarded and that each person has a chance to achieve success in life out of her own commitment and hard work are characterized by a low demand for income transfer. On the contrary, countries where individuals believe that economic conditions are more a matter of luck and connections and that people have little chances of achieving success in life on the basis of their effort and commitment are those where there is an high demand for redistribution. The extent to which people believe that the process of wealth and poverty formation is fair is crucially dependent on their level of autonomy freedom.

The relationship between autonomy freedom and welfare spending allowed us to construct a taxonomy of welfare systems in the OECD countries. We demonstrated that, with the only exceptions of Turkey and Japan, the principle of procedural fairness affects government redistributive policies in OECD countries.

8

Choice, Freedom, and the Good Society

The last chapter in a book is almost obliged to offer a summary of the arguments tackled and deployed in the pages that precede. In the case at hand, the obligation is inescapable as the journey has been long and across disciplines. We do not want to dodge such duties. Yet, we feel that an important aspect – albeit one that cannot be exhausted here – of our measure of freedom is still open. This has to do with its contribution to the design of a satisfactory view of liberalism and a good society.

The accomplishment of this final task cannot be eschewed if we want to provide a complete picture of the effort undertaken in these pages. After all, the value of developing a measure of freedom must extend beyond the measure itself to involve considerations that embrace, first and foremost, a view of liberalism and a good society. However, a fully fledged prescriptive picture would require the deployment of an argument for which adequate space – and probably even the reader's patience – is not available, at this point. We then limit ourselves to a simple sketch of the view of liberalism that our interpretation of autonomy freedom entails. To this end, we exploit a powerful tool: the reasons why choice is valuable. Such a tool turns out to be incredibly flexible. The rankings of choice introduced in the first part of the book can be interpreted in the light of the value that each of them attributes to choice. We are then in a position to sketch the view of liberalism that our interpretation of autonomy freedom entails and, at the same time, to fulfill the obligation that rests with the last chapter of any book, to offer a summary of the arguments and avenues for future research.

Recall where we departed from, in Chapters 2 and 3: the search for a measure of freedom that could complement the information provided by the existing empirical rods and that could also be grounded on firm conceptual foundations. The result is our theoretical measure of autonomy freedom and its empirical counterpart, developed in Chapter 4. Such a result is intimately dependent upon a particular reason for valuing choice that we labeled *procedural*. It is just the procedural importance of choice that separates our measure from the other existing rods and that entails the conclusions on the design of liberalism and a good society that we are going to outline in this final chapter.

Armed with such a reason for attributing value to choice, we return to the relations that our measure entertains with the other theoretical and empirical rods of freedom touched upon in this book, in the next section. We are able to show where our measure stands and, interestingly, also to expose some of the difficulties the other rods experience in terms of some values highly held in the preceding pages such as diversity and responsibility. The first limit, by and large, pertains to the empirical measure of economic freedom, whereas the latter applies to Sen's idea of capability and functionings. In the last section, we exploit in full the gains offered by our powerful tool (i.e., the reasons why choice is valuable). In particular, we construct a simple analytical frame that describes the overall level of freedom in a given society. Such a frame allows us to present an outline of our view of liberalism and the good society.

8.1 FREEDOM AND THE VALUE OF CHOICE

Intrinsic Importance of Choice and Economic Freedom

Time and again, this book has stressed a particular interpretation of the value of choice that constitutes the central pillar of our argument. Drawing from the Millian framework canvassed in the third chapter of *On Liberty*, we have attributed value to choice for *procedural* reasons. Accordingly, having alternatives to choose from is valuable for its effects on the process that leads a decision maker to undertake a specific course of action or to select a given option. In other words, availability of choices enriches the deliberative process and, in the typical

Millian spirit, contributes to the development and exercise of individuality (or autonomy). A person whose course in life has been shaped out of choices that are outcomes of deliberative processes where she has crafted her preferences on the basis of a careful weighing of the pros and cons of alternative courses of action and consciously relying upon her personal and moral values is a person who is fully accountable for her decisions and, in this peculiar sense, autonomous. Such a person is likely to design the course of her life in a unique fashion that reflects her particular and unrepeatable set of values, skills, convictions and objectives, making herself a fully conscious and thinking being.

The procedural importance of choice marks a distance with respect to the other existing measures, both at the theoretical and at the empirical level. Simple cardinality, which is probably the closest ranking we may think of to the Berlinian view of negative freedom,[1] attributes intrinsic importance to choice and characterizes the measure in terms of alternative sets of opportunities that a decision maker has *the power to achieve*. Choice is relevant in this case because the act of choosing delivers a more pregnant meaning to what a person achieves, even if the achievement was unaffected by lack of choice.

The same can be said for the empirical measures of economic freedom. Based upon objective statistical information and a firm reliance on the idea of negative freedom, they do not explicitly dwell on the reasons for valuing choice but, if pressed, would probably agree that choice is valuable for intrinsic and instrumental reasons and that the freedom they measure is, as in SCO, the power to achieve. We believe so because both the *Economic Freedom of the World* (EFW) Index and the Heritage Foundation's *Index of Economic Freedom* are, in our view, measures of limited government. In other words, what they assess is the extent to which free markets are complemented, in a given country, by government institutions under the rule of law to ensure undistorted choice to decision makers. In so doing, they subscribe to the view, canvassed mainly by Milton Friedman, that choice is important as it reflects the view that freedom consists of the affirmation of individuality and diversity in society.

---

[1] We do not intend to make an explicit case here. It suffices to observe that Berlin mentions the extent of possibilities open for choice to a decision maker as one of the criteria on the basis of which freedom should be quantified.

Consider a standard demand–supply microeconomic model that describes a perfectly competitive market. The role attributed to governmental institutions is limited to the enforcement of property rights. Each agent obtains (or offers) exactly as many units of the good as his marginal valuation requires, given the prevailing price level. No distortion exists on the decision makers' choices and the widest possibility for diversity is ensured since each agent responds to his marginal valuation, which, in turn, depends upon his unique structure of preferences. Under these circumstances economic freedom is the widest, and no reference *seems* necessary to the procedural value of choice. Choosing is valuable for intrinsic reasons (as in SCO, since choosing is better than not) as well as instrumental, since it fosters diversity. As we will see in the next section, although the approach has merits, the relationship between choice and diversity is more complicated than what the simple microeconomic model allows us to see. More precisely, diversity can be derived from free-market exchanges only if choice is also valued for its procedural consequences.

Capabilities, Functionings, and the Value of Choice

A similar no-show story for the procedural value of choice may be told with reference to the measure of positive freedom proposed by Amartya Sen. An account of his view must move from the acknowledgment that his interest on the extent of freedom a person enjoys springs from his attempt to assess that person's position in a social arrangement. Sen correctly argues that the focus on achievements that dominates economic analysis leads to unpalatable moral conclusions. He looks with favor to the Rawlsian concern with the distribution of primary goods or to the Dworkinian attention to the distribution of resources as these approaches walk away from exclusive reliance on achievements. Nonetheless, he thinks that neither of them covers the distance that leads to an adequate assessment of the extent of freedom since neither of them assesses well-being in the appropriate space.

Well-being, according to Sen (1992), must be judged on the basis of the quality of functionings a person enjoys since the latter are "constitutive of a person's being". At the same time, a person's *capability to function* "represents the various combinations of functionings [...] that the person can achieve" (p. 40). Accordingly, capability reflects the person's freedom to lead the kind of life she has reason to value. Freedom must then be assessed in the space of capabilities and is composed by two dimensions, each of them linked to a particular interpretation of the value of choice. Freedom has to do with access to alternative sets of accomplishments (capability sets) that we have *the power to achieve* and, at the same time, that we *value to achieve*. If freedom is related to the power to achieve and its assessment depends on the capability set (the set of functionings), the well-being of a person takes into account the *opportunity freedom* to promote or achieve what she values doing or being. In this case, the value of choice is intrinsic in the sense that it does not depend on the outcome of the process of choice. On the contrary, if freedom is related to what we may achieve, then the value of choice is instrumental: It allows us to attain those functionings that we have reason to value.

Sen's treatment of the value of choice makes neither reference to the procedural dimension of valuing choice nor to the fact that deliberating entails responsibility and, eventually, autonomy. This is not a minor difference that can be appreciated only within academic circles. Take the World Value Survey question *A173* that represents the empirical counterpart of the theoretical measure of autonomy freedom proposed in this book. Such a question refers explicitly to freedom of choice and control, and we have repeatedly asserted (see mainly Chapter 4) that the combination of these two ingredients yields a quantitative account of people's autonomy freedom. On the contrary, the more favorable evaluation in terms of well-being of a larger capability set derives, according to Sen (1992), either from the fact that (1) choosing is a "valuable part of living, and a life of genuine choice with serious options may be seen to be – for that reason – richer" (p. 41) or from (2) achieving those functionings that the person has reasons to value. If we were (hypothetically) reformulating the WVS question *A173* to accommodate Sen's interpretation of the value of choice, it should assess *how much freedom of choice and control a person has to achieve what she has reasons to value.*

The distance between the original and the hypothetical formulation of *A173* should not be overlooked. The latter assigns no role to personal responsibility and does not provide adequate room for eccentricity since the reasons to value do not necessarily entail a rich deliberative process. An example offered by Sugden (2006) may illustrate our point.

Consider two states of the world: {x}, described as "exposed to danger of malaria" and, {y}, described as "not exposed to danger of malaria". Note that, since eradication of malaria is a typical public good brought about by collective action at the national or international level, a single decision maker has no (or a fairly limited) role to play. If we were measuring the extent of freedom with the hypothetical *A173* question, we would expect respondents to say, in fact, that {y} delivers greater freedom than {x} since

[b]eing able to live as one would value, desire and choose *is* a contribution to one's freedom. (Sen, 1992, p. 68)

On the contrary, if exposed to the standard formulation of question *A173*, which captures control, respondents would likely rank the two states as indifferent in terms of freedom since neither of them requires any reference to the deliberative process that develops and fosters autonomy.

In conclusion, we believe that our emphasis on the procedural value of choice leads to an original measure of freedom that is separated from the existing rods, both at the theoretical and empirical level. Furthermore, the procedural value may usefully complement the intrinsic, leading to a more satisfactory account of freedom and a more accurate measurement than the account and the measure so far proposed by the economic freedom rod and its theoretical underpinnings. The benefits of an accurate measurement fall on both the interpretive and the prescriptive analysis of freedom, as the last section argues. Beforehand, we want to illustrate the sense in which the complementary role of the procedural and the substantive value of choice may yield a more satisfactory account of freedom.

8.2 CHOICE, VOLUNTARINESS, AND DIVERSITY

Complementing Economic Freedom

It is understandable – yet surprising – that the received wisdom of liberalism, embodied by the negative freedom view, has paid no more than lip service to the procedural value of choice. One way to make sense of such a neglect, suggested by Ian Carter in the *Stanford Encyclopedia of Philosophy*, is that "theorists of negative freedom are primarily interested in the degree to which individuals or groups suffer interference from external bodies, [while] theorists of positive freedom are more attentive to the internal factors affecting the degree to which individuals [...] act autonomously." The received wisdom of liberalism interprets focusing on the internal factors as a betrayal of the *true* concept of freedom since it carries with it the danger of authoritarianism. The reasons for such a fear have extensively been explored by Berlin: They hinge upon the consequences of faith in the identification of the true self and its implications in the design of a society for those unprepared to conform to the true self.

We find the sharp distinction between positive and negative freedom artificial and damaging for a satisfactory measurement of freedom both at the theoretical and empirical level. Political philosophers have filled innumerable pages to stigmatize the distinction and to defend one way or another to bridge it. We have no intention to provide an argument in support of any further "third way" between the negative and positive face of the notion of freedom.[2] With Berlin, we believe that they are not at a great logical distance from each other just like two sides of the same medal.[3] The interest this book shows on such a distance depends upon our concern about freedom measurement and is rooted in the claim that a measure like autonomy freedom, which privileges the internal factors, successfully complements rods exclusively based on the "standard view" of negative freedom. We suggest that (but we do not argue for, strictly speaking) combining the two measures delivers a better quantitative understanding partly because it provides a more satisfactory picture of liberalism than that offered by a mere negative freedom–based view.

We have repeatedly asserted in this book that all the available measures of freedom are connected to choice and can be distinguished on the basis of the value that they attribute to the act of choosing. By disregarding the procedural value of choice, the measure of economic freedom might not deliver what it promises. In *The Limits of*

---

[2] Plenty of arguments for a third way are available in the boundless philosophical literature on freedom. Any account would be unfair as it it is doomed to be incomplete. As an example, we may direct the reader to the idea of "republican freedom" advanced by Philip Pettit (1997, 2001).

[3] At least, if one considers Berlin's interpretation of positive freedom that should not be conflated with Sen's.

Liberty, Buchanan writes that "the free market offers maximal scope for private, personal eccentricity, for individual freedom in its most elementary meaning" (Buchanan, 1975, p. 18). Such a view is by no means isolated: Milton Friedman, who, by the way, inspired the construction of the *Economic Freedom of the World Index*, in *Capitalism and Freedom*, argues at length that market exchanges allow the affirmation of personal eccentricity and (hence) diversity in society, as the following passage explicitly states:

The characteristic feature of action through political channels is that it tends to require or enforce substantial conformity. The great advantage of the market, on the other hand, is that it permits wide diversity. It is, in political terms, a system of proportional representation. Each man can vote, as it were, for the color of the tie he wants and get it; he does not have to see what color the majority wants and then, if he is in the minority, submit.

It is this feature of the market we refer to when we say that the market provides economic freedom. (Friedman, 1962, p. 15)

Buchanan and Friedman's are forceful defenses of negative freedom. What they claim is that the exercise of choice or the manifestation of one's will (allowed by the unfettered functioning of market mechanisms) lead to personal eccentricity or the affirmation of diversity in society, namely the affirmation of (negative) freedom in its most elementary meaning. In their perspective, the free market is the most suited institutional environment where choice may be exercised, where eccentricity has a chance to prevail. This is entirely agreeable. But, what it should not be overlooked is that the exercise of choice and the affirmation of diversity are two components of negative freedom that, unfortunately, might depart each other if not assisted by the powerful glue provided by autonomy. In other words, voluntariness (i.e., the exercise of choice) and diversity (i.e., the manifestation of eccentricity) might go in opposite ways if the realization of the former is heteronymous.

To clarify, negative freedom can be considered as composed by two elements. On the one hand, voluntariness or the exercise of choice; on the other, diversity or eccentricity. In the received wisdom cast by the negative freedom tradition, voluntariness is a sufficient condition for the affirmation of diversity or eccentricity. But this is at best a statistical claim as things can easily be more complicated: If the manifestation of voluntariness is not assisted by autonomy, diversity may still exist but it might be the product of mere chance. In fact, it cannot logically be excluded that a (negatively) free society might show complete uniformity and that eccentricity is not realized.

The index of economic freedom reflects such a difficulty. It fares well at capturing voluntariness but runs into troubles if called to the assessment of diversity. The latest summary rating available for the *Economic Freedom of the World* (EFW) rod lists Singapore among the freest country in the world despite the undemocratic politics of the regime that governs the city-state. The peculiar listing of Singapore rings a bell that deserves readier ears than those offered so far. In many circumstances, markets give the possibility for personal – or even eccentric – choices but people may select what they buy to conform to social customs or to the pressure exercised by their peers in the social circumstances in which they find themselves. John Stuart Mill used to chastise his fellow countrymen for their thoughtless adherence to the Victorian customs prevailing in his days, and British citizens had already a system of allocation of resources mainly based on market exchanges with limited scope and role for the state, especially by contemporary standards.

These two examples suggest that the index of economic freedom is surely more a rod for voluntariness than for the diversity dimension of negative freedom. Such a fundamental component of negative freedom seems left out of an explicit calculation and the missing information is relevant. It is just in this gap that our measure may contribute. By giving explicit voice to the procedural value of choice, it assesses autonomous behavior and the affirmation of diversity. Heterogeneity and eccentricity – which would otherwise be merely assumed by the economic freedom rods – can now be quantified, making full justice of the meaning of economic freedom expressed by the Friedman's quotation reported earlier. And the benefits extend beyond measurement of economic freedom to involve an understanding of liberalism that is, at least, more realistic and defensible, as the next section maintains.

Diversity and the Capability Approach

As we have argued, the procedural value of choice marks a substantial difference in the measurement of freedom also with respect to

Sen's capability approach. The difference involves the *potential* policy consequences of the two approaches. An illustration which brings to the forefront the value of choice and that we subscribe to is provided by Sugden (2006). According to Sugden, a central component (at least from the perspective of policies) of Sen's theory of well-being is reasoned evaluation. The instrumental value that Sen assigns to functionings requires a criterion that establishes their value. Recourse to utilitarianism is foreclosed by the inadequateness of "the mental metric of pleasure or desire" in assigning correct weights (and therefore values) to different functionings. What Sen is left with is then to invoke a concept of reason that is as universal as possible.

Note that Mill, who subscribes to the procedural value of choice, faces a similar problem. In Sugden's reading, Mill too is skeptical about "the mental metric of pleasure or desire" in the sense that it can hardly be considered as evidence of what is good for a person. Yet, Mill does not appeal to reasoned evaluation to assign value to opportunities. More than that: since he deems choice as valuable for procedural reasons, he simply does not need to rely upon any substantive value of the available options. On the contrary, "he advocates general rules which allow each individual as much freedom as possible to choose between alternative ways – good, bad or indifferent – of living her own life" (p. 43) since these rules are the only ones that may ensure the realization of a person's individuality.

If portrayed in these terms, the difference between Mill and Sen might appear of little practical significance. In fact, it is not, as it bears major consequences for policy design. Once we appeal to reasoned evaluation, at the political level we must construct what Sugden properly calls "some kind of reasoned 'consensus' " on how to value the available functionings. In other words, if choice is valuable for what it allows to achieve, society must decide what is valuable to achieve. Since Sen is careful to reject imposed evaluation – after all, he also attributes intrinsic value to choice – he must appeal to some kind of democratic consensus that can only be achieved via a collective judgment process. The reference here is not necessarily to a voting system since the consensus may or may not overlap with what the majority values. But, however it is achieved, the relevant question from our perspective is whether, under any given democratic consensus, a person is entitled to live the kind of life she desires, *whatever that may be*. The problem with Sen's treatment of the value of choice is that the answer to this question is not necessarily in the positive. With Sugden (2006), we fear that Sen's proposal might license

collective decisions that override some individuals' actual desires about how to live their own lives, in favor of other people's judgements about what those individuals have reasons to desire. (p. 41)

We are not claiming that this is doomed to happen in Sen's theory, nor that it is likely. We are simply saying that it cannot logically be ruled out and that is enough – in our view – to reject his treatment of the value of choice.

On the contrary, once procedural value is attributed to choice, and, as a consequence, all opportunities contribute to the development of individuality, we do not need to rely upon any "external" (albeit impartial or universal) consensus to assign weights but only upon whatever each person *might* (the reference here is to counterfactual choice) desire. The difference in terms of policy between the two approaches cannot be underestimated. Mill's view of the value of choice is compatible with a society in which the scope for personal choice and eccentricity is guaranteed, in which the affirmation of individual freedom in its most elementary meaning (to return to Buchanan) is not prejudiced. And this is enough, in our view, to defend the procedural understanding of the value of choice and to enfranchise our view of freedom and its policy consequences as Sugden's quotation reproduced below exemplifies:

What is at issue here can be expressed in terms of the familiar case of the "contented slave." [...] The problem is this: if slaves are contented, on what grounds can we condemn slavery? If we use a metric of actual desire, there seems to be nothing to criticize. Sen's approach is to ask whether the contented slave has reason to desire a different way of life, from which she is debarred by her slavery. In contrast, Mill's approach is to ask what would happen if the slave ceased to be contented: if she came to desire a different way of life, could she walk away from her existing one? Sen's approach leads to a critique of slavery that can be opposed by those who claim that slaves have no reason to value a life outside slavery. [...] In contrast, Mill's argument retains its force against opponents who claim exactly this. If these opponents really believe what they say, what have they to fear from the abolition of slavery? If the slaves are so contented, why do they need to be prevented from walking away? (2006, p. 46)

8.3 THE FREEDOMS' BOX

We wish to propose one further perspective on the complementarity of our measure of freedom with respect to the economic freedom rods as well as one further distinction with respect to Sen's notion of positive freedom. A perspective that allows us to illustrate the consequences of our measure of autonomy freedom for a view of liberalism. To do that, we start with the introduction of a simple analytical tool, the "freedoms' box", depicted in Figure 8.1, which shows the overall level of freedom in a given society.

On the horizontal axis, we measure the level of negative freedom as captured by the extent of government intervention (as expressed, for example, by one of the economic freedom rods). Of course, the wider negative freedom, the lower government intervention, up to a point, denoted by *A* in the bottom-right corner of the figure, where the level of negative freedom is that guaranteed by the minimal state. Given the institutional structure of the country represented in the freedoms' box, point *A* indicates the maximum attainable level of negative freedom and may change across countries. On the vertical axis, we place either the level of autonomy freedom as measured by our rod or that of positive freedom (i.e., the extent of opportunities), quantified by Sen's approach to freedom.

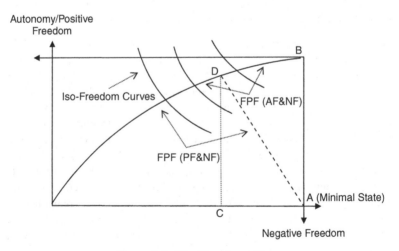

Figure 8.1. The Freedoms' Box.

Both negative freedom and autonomy freedom are "goods" since it is reasonable to expect that they benefit the individual who would rather have more of both than less, and they are complementary, as our discussion has shown. Drawing a parallel with standard economics, we can then trace a positive sloping *freedom possibility frontier* which associates to each level of negative freedom the maximum amount of autonomy freedom that a society may enjoy. Since the freedom possibility frontier has a positive slope, a move from the bottom-left to the top-right corner of the figure reflects an increase in the total level of freedom in society, the area underneath the frontier. It follows that the maximum attainable level of negative and autonomy freedom in a society is given by the area delimited by the origin, on the one side, and points *B* in the top-right corner of the figure and *A*, in the bottom-right.

However, if we consider negative and positive freedom, the shape of the frontier changes as the latter is not complementary to the former and, if the negative dimension overcomes a given (country specific) limit, it depresses positive freedom. In other words, we are assuming that beyond a certain limit, an increase in negative freedom comes at the expenses of positive freedom since they become substitutes. This assumption is consistent with Sen's approach, as he says that negative freedom can coexist with lack of access to opportunity. The conflict between these two interpretations of freedom does not appear, though, for low levels of negative freedom as it is reasonable to expect that intrusive governments distort choice and reduce its extent, too. Typically, conflict emerges when certain functionings that are considered nonreducible for the attainment of a decent life cannot be accessed. We may imagine that, in the country depicted in Figure 8.1, the trade-off between negative and positive freedom starts at point *C*. Hence, Sen's freedom possibility frontier is monotonically increasing up to *C* and decreases all the way down to point *A*. Consistently, the downward-sloping shape of the second part of the freedom possibility frontier indicates a trade-off between positive and negative freedom and that the maximum level of freedom attainable in this society is given by the quasi-triangular shape delimited by the origin, on the one side, and points *D* and *A*, on the other.

What the freedoms' box illustrates is twofold. First, it shows the complementarity between autonomy freedom and negative freedom. In

Figure 8.1 such a complementarity derives from the previous section's argument that voluntariness and diversity are two separate dimensions of negative freedom that have to be considered jointly, for the benefit of the analysis and measurement of freedom as well as for its affirmation. The practical consequence of this complementarity is that the array of policies that can be designed to advance liberty expands without being exposed to the risk that Sen's prescriptions may incur. The array expands to the extent that these policies involve, beyond the retreat of the state, the increase of responsibility and the possibility to develop eccentric ways to affirm one's personality in life.

Second, and more interestingly, the freedoms' box takes an evident normative stance: A good society is that where negative and autonomy freedom are maximal, as indicated by point *B*. Its normative position has interesting implications for liberalism. To start with, it does not suffice to maximize negative freedom. If in a given society the extent of government is reduced, the freedoms' box requires that autonomy freedom crowds in. Consider the following example. Significant cuts to public expenditure have recently been introduced in many countries in Western Europe to balance the budget. Even though they reduce the dimension of government and increase negative freedom, they might not be able to increase overall freedom unless they are accompanied by policies that do not depress the level of autonomy freedom. These policies do not necessarily require greater state intervention, but they are likely to involve the design of institutional frameworks in which people may spontaneously undertake initiatives that fill the space left empty by the public hand.[4]

Note the interplay of two dimensions of freedom in the previous example. Such an interplay opens the way to another important difference that autonomy freedom imposes on our view of liberalism: a greater degree of discretion that policy makers enjoy to foster the affirmation of overall freedom. An important practical consequence is that limited government may be reduced by increasing autonomy freedom.

---

[4] A typical example is Hayek's *indirect* intervention of the state, namely an intervention whose sole aim is to delineate the frame in which individuals may pursue their private interests.

This is because a rise in the level of autonomy freedom makes people more responsible and less eager to use the public hand to redress inequality or, in general, to solve their problems.

Furthermore, our more refined liberalism prescribes that, as negative freedom increases, a good society should substitute state intervention in support of the needy with private commitment. This claim can be read in different ways. For example, in terms of the argument highlighted in the previous chapter, it says that among the procedurally fair countries, some are more desirable societies than others. These are the societies that lie in the lower-right quadrant of Figure 7.2, where negative freedom is high and, at the same time, autonomy is likely to create the conditions for the affirmation of an active society in which social protection is guaranteed by private intervention. Another interpretation of this prescriptive claim would be that a good society is that where public goods are privately provided. This is because, in the spirit of Milton Friedman, private solutions are tailored to individual needs in a way that public solutions are not. As a consequence, not only do they foster diversity, but they also satisfy preferences more accurately or, in the language of this book, favor achievements.

Finally, a society made up of autonomous persons is likely to be a good society from one further perspective. Intuition suggests that if autonomy freedom flourishes, so do civic virtues. The reason might be that autonomous persons should be able to overcome the many conflicts that life in society poses more easily than nonautonomous persons. That should favor the construction of the social fabric that is necessary for civic virtues to affirm themselves. We make no secret that reference to civic virtues pushes our normative claim toward conservative shores. We are not referring here to the policies and ideological positions adopted by political parties who bear the label "conservative." Quite contrarily, we are thinking of the idea – cherished by the British conservatism embodied in the work of Michael Oakeshott or Michael Polanyi – that traditions are important to the making of a good society. Of course, there is a tension between the Millian search for eccentricity and the procedural value of choice that we have defended in these pages and the conservative disposition in favor of the status quo. How this tension might be resolved here we cannot say.

Nonetheless, we believe that a society that realizes the maximum level of overall freedom (i.e., negative and autonomy freedom) must be a society characterized by limited state intervention, a high degree of personal realization, and some kind of conservative disposition. How these three ingredients should best be combined to achieve what we think is the good society, is something for another book to search and, hopefully, to answer.

Bibliography

Alergi, R., and J. Nieto (2001a): "Incomplete preferences and the preference for flexibility," *Mathematical Social Sciences*, 41, 151–65.

———— (2001b): "Ranking opportunity sets: An approach based on the preference for flexibility," *Social Choice and Welfare*, 18, 23–36.

Alesina, A., and G. M. Angeletos (2005): "Fairness and redistribution," *American Economic Review*, 95, 960–80.

Alesina, A., and A. Drazen (1991): "Why are stabilizations delayed?," *American Economic Review*, 81, 1170–88.

Alesina, A., and N. Fuchs-Schündeln (2007): "Good-Bye Lenin (or not?): The effect of communism on people's preferences," *American Economic Review*, 97, 1507–28.

Alesina, A., and E. La Ferrara (2001): "Participation in heterogeneous communities," *Quarterly Journal of Economics*, 115, 847–904.

———— (2005): "Redistribution in the land of opportunity," *Journal of Public Economics*, 89, 897–931.

Alesina, A., and E. L. Glaeser (2004): *Fighting Poverty in the US and Europe: A World of Difference*. Oxford University Press, Oxford.

Alesina, A., and D. Rodrik (1994): "Distributive politics and economic growth," *Quarterly Journal of Economics*, 109, 465–90.

Alesina, A., and R. Wacziarg (1998): "Openness, country size and the government," *Journal of Public Economics*, 69, 305–22.

Alesina, A., A. Devleeschauwer, W. Easterly, S. Kurlat, and R. Wacziarg (2003): "Fractionalization," *Journal of Economic Growth*, 8, 155–94.

Alesina, A., E. L. Glaeser, and B. Sacerdote (2001): "Why doesn't the US have a European-style welfare state," *Brookings Papers on Economic Activity*, Fall, 187–277.

Banting, Keith, Richard Johnston, Will Kymlicka and Stuart Soroka (2006): "Do Multiculturalism Policies Erode the Welfare State? An Empirical

Analysis," in *Multiculturalism and the Welfare State*, ed. by Keith Banting and Will Kymlicka. Oxford University Press, Oxford.

Barrotta, P. (2008): "Why economists should be unhappy with the economics of happiness," *Economics and Philosophy*, 24, 145–65.

Bartels, L. M. (1996): "Uninformed votes: Information effects in presidential campaigns," *American Journal of Political Science*, 40, 194–230.

Bavetta, S. (2004): "Measuring freedom of choice: An alternative view of a recent literature," *Social Choice and Welfare*, 22, 29–48.

Bavetta, S., and M. Del Seta (2001): "Constraints and the measurement of freedom of choice," *Theory and Decision*, 50, 213–38.

Bavetta, S., and F. Guala (2003): "Autonomy freedom and deliberation," *Journal of Theoretical Politics*, 15, 423–43.

———— (2009): "Opportunity and Individuality," Mimeo.

Bavetta, S., and V. Peragine (2006): "Measuring autonomy freedom," *Social Choice and Welfare*, 26, 31–45.

Bavetta, S. and P. Navarra (2004): "Theoretical Foundations of an Empirical Measure of Freedom: A Research Challenge to Liberal Economists," *Economic Affairs*, 24, 44–46.

Bavetta, S., A. Cognata, D. Maimone Ansaldo Patti, and P. Navarra (2008): "Individual control in decision-making and attitudes toward inequality: The case of Italy," in *Power: Conceptual, Formal and Applied Dimensions*, ed. by M. Braham and F. Steffen, pp. 343–64. Springer, Berlin.

Bénabou, R., and E. A. Ok (2001): "Social mobility and the demand for redistribution: The POUM hypothesis," *Quarterly Journal of Economics*, 116, 447–87.

Bénabou, R., and J. Tirole (2006): "Belief in a just world and redistributive politics," *Quarterly Journal of Economics*, 121, 699–746.

Benhabib, J., and A. Rustichini (1991): "Vintage capital, investment and growth," *Journal of Economic Theory*, 55, 323–39.

Berlin, I. (1969): *Four Essays on Liberty*. Oxford University Press, Oxford.

Bethencourt Marrero, C., and V. Galasso (2001): "On the Political Complementarity Between Health Care and Social Security," CEPR Discussion Papers 2788.

Birdsall, N., D. Ross, and R. H. Sabot (1995): "Inequality and growth reconsidered. Lessons from East Asia," *World Bank Economic Review*, 9, 477–508.

Bjørnskov, Christian (2006): "Determinants of Generalized Trust: A Cross-Country Comparison," *Public Choice*, 130, 1–21.

Boeri, T., I. J. Conde-Ruiz, and V. Galasso (2003): "Protecting Against Labour Market Risk: Employment Protection or Unemployment Benefits?," CEPR Discussion Paper No. 3990.

Boldrin, M., and A. Montes (2005): "The intergenerational state: public education and pensions," *Review of Economic Studies*, 72, 651–64.

Borges, J. L. (1974): *Ficciones*. Emecé Editores, Madrid, Alianza Editorial, 1994.

Bossert, W. (1997): "Opportunity sets and individual well-being," *Social Choice and Welfare*, 14, 97–112.

Bossert, W., P. K. Pattanaik, and Y. Xu (1994): "Ranking opportunity sets: An axiomatic approach," *Journal of Economic Theory*, 63, 326–45.

——— (2003): "Similarity of options and the measurement of diversity," *Journal of Theoretical Politics*, 15, 405–21.

Bradley, D., E. Huber, S. Moller, F. Nielsen, and J. D. Stephens (2003): "Distribution and Redistribution in Postindustrial Democracies," *World Politics*, 55, 193–228.

Breyer, F., and H. Ursprung (1998): "Are the rich too rich to be expropriated? Economic power and the feasibility of constitutional limits to redistribution," *Public Choice*, 94, 135–56.

Buchanan, J. (1975): *The Limits of Liberty. Between Anarchy and Leviathan*. University of Chicago Press, Chicago.

Buchanan, J. M., and G. Tullock (1962): *The Calculus of Consent. Logical Foundations of Constitutional Democracy*. University of Michigan Press, Ann Arbor.

Carter, I. (1999): *A Measure of Freedom*. Oxford University Press, Oxford.

——— (2004): "Choice, freedom and freedom of choice," *Social Choice and Welfare*, 22, 61–81.

Chomsky, N., and E. S. Herman (1988): *Manufacturing Consent. the Political Economy of Mass Media*. Pantheon, New York.

Coate, S., and S. Morris (1995): "On the form of transfers to special interests," *Journal of Political Economy*, 103, 1210–35.

Cole, H. L., G. J. Mailath, and A. Postlewaite (1992): "Social norms, savings behavior, and growth," *Journal of Political Economy*, 100, 1092–125.

Conde-Ruiz, I. J., and V. Galasso (2003): "Early retirement," *Review of Economic Dynamics*, 6, 12–36.

Corneo, G., and H. P. Grüner (2000): "Social limits to redistribution," *American Economic Review*, 90, 1491–1507.

——— (2002): "Individual preferences for political redistribution," *Journal of Public Economics*, 83, 83–107.

Deci, E. L., and R. Flaste (1995): *Why We Do What We Do. The Dynamics of Personal Autonomy*. Putnam, New York.

Deci, E. L., and R. M. Ryan (1985): *Intrinsic Motivation and Self-Determination in Human Behavior*. Plenum Press, New York.

Deci, E. L., R. Koestner, and R. M. Ryan (1999): "A meta-analytic review of extrinsic rewards on intrinsic motivation," *Psychological Bullettin*, 125, 627–68.

Dougan, W. R., and J. M. Snyder (1993): "Are Rents Fully Dissipated?," *Public Choice*, 77, 793–813.

Douglas, M. T., and A. B. Wildavsky (1983): *Risk and Culture. An Essay on the Selection of Technical and Environmental Dangers*. University of California Press, Berkeley.

Dowding, K., and P. John (2009): "The value of choice in public policy," *Public Administration*, 87, 219–33.

Dowding, K., and M. van Hees (2009): "Freedom of choice," in *Oxford Handbook of Rational and Social Choice*, ed. by P. Anand, C. Puppe, and P. K. Pattanaik, pp. 374–92. Oxford University Press, Oxford.

Eisenberger, R., L. Rhoades, and J. Cameron (1999): "Does pay for performance increase or decrease perceived self-determination and intrinsic motivation?," *Journal of Personality and Social Psychology*, 64, 1026–40.

Epple, D., and T. Romer (1991): "Mobility and redistribution," *Journal of Political Economy*, 99, 828–58.

Falk, A., and M. Kosfeld (2006): "Distrust – The hidden cost of control," *American Economic Review*, 96, 1611–30.

Fearon, J. D. (2003): "Ethnic and cultural diversity by country," *Journal of Economic Growth*, 8, 195–222.

Fernandez, R., and R. Rogerson (1995): "On the political economy of education subsidy," *Review of Economic Studies*, 62, 249–62.

Ferrer-i Carbonell, A., and P. Frijters (2004): "How important is methodology for the estimates of the determinants of happiness?," *The Economic Journal*, 114, 641–59.

Foner, E. (1998): *The Story of American Freedom*. Norton, New York.

Fong, C. (2001): "Social preferences, self-interest, and the demand for redistribution," *Journal of Public Economics*, 82, 225–46.

——— (2006): "Prospective Mobility, Fairness, and the Demand for Redistribution," Mimeo, University of Pittsburgh.

Frey, B. (1997): *Not Just for the Money: An Economic Theory of Personal Motivation*. Edward Elgar, Cheltenham.

Frey, B. S., and A. Stutzer (2002): *Happiness and Economics. How the Economy and Institutions Affect Well-Being*. Princeton University Press, Princeton.

Frey, B., M. Benz, and A. Stutzer (2004): "Introducing procedural utility: Not only what, but also how matters," *Journal of Institutional and Theoretical Economics*, 160, 377–401.

Friedman, M. (1962): *Capitalism and Freedom*. University of Chicago Press, Chicago.

Friedman, M. and R. Friedman (1980): *Free to Choose: A Personal Statement*, San Diego: Harcourt.

Galasso, V., and P. Profeta (2002): "The political economy of social security: A survey," *European Journal of Political Economy*, 18, 1–29.

Gravel, N. (1998): "Ranking opportunity sets on the basis of their freedom of choice and their ability to satisfy preferences: A difficulty," *Social Choice and Welfare*, 15, 371–82.

Gray, J. (1996): *Mill on Liberty: A Defence*. Routledge, London.

Greene, W. H. (2007): *Econometric Analysis*. Prentice-Hall, Upper Saddle River.

Guiso, L., P. Sapienza, and L. Zingales (2003): "People's opium? Religion and economic attitudes," *Journal of Monetary Economics*, 50, 225–82.

Gwartney, J., R. Lawson and J. Hall (2011): *Economic Freedom of the World: 2011 Annual Report*. Fraser Institute, Vancouver.

Harms, P., and S. Zink (2003): "Limits to redistribution in a democray: A survey," *European Journal of Political Economy*, 19, 651–68.

Hausman, J., and D. McFadden (1984): "Specification tests for the multinomial logit model," *Econometrica*, 52, 1219–40.

Hayek, F. A. (1960): *The Constitution of Liberty*. Routledge and Kegan Paul, London.

Hero, Rodney (2003): "Multiple Traditions in American Politics and Racial Policy Inequality," *Political Research Quarterly*, 56, 401–408.

Hirschman, A. O. (1973): "The changing tolerance for income inequality in the course of economic development," *Quarterly Journal of Economics*, 87, 544–66.

Hobbes, T. (1990): *Leviathan*. Cambridge University Press, Cambridge.

Inglehart, R. F., and C. Welzel (2005): *Modernization, Cultural Change and Democracy*. Cambridge University Press, Cambridge.

Iversen, T. (2005): *Capitalism, Democracy and Welfare*. Cambridge University Press, Cambridge.

Iversen, T., and D. Soskice (2006): "Electoral institutions and the politics of coalitions: Why some democracies redistribute more than others," *American Political Science Review*, 100, 165–81.

Jones, P., and R. Sugden (1982): "Evaluating choice," *International Review of Law and Economics*, 12, 47–65.

Kahneman, D., P. P. Wakker, and S. Rakesh (1997): "Back to Bentham? Explorations of experienced utility," *Quarterly Journal of Economics*, 112, 375–405.

Kalyvas, S. N. (1996): *The Rise of Christian Democracy in Europe*. Cornell University Press, Ithaca.

Kitschelt, H. (1994): *The Transformation of European Social Democracy*. Cambridge University Press, Cambridge.

Klemisch-Alhert, M. (1993): "Freedom of Choice: A Comparison of Different Rankings of Opportunity Sets," *Social Choice and Welfare*, 10, 189–207.

Kreps, D. M. (1979): "A Representation Theorem for 'Preference for Flexibility'," *Econometrica*, 47, 565–77.

Kristov, L., P. Lindert, and R. McClelland (1992): "Pressure groups and redistribution," *Journal of Public Economics*, 48, 153–63.

Lane, R. E. (1959): "Fear of equality," *American Political Science Review*, 59, 35–51.

Langfred, C. W. (2005): "Autonomy and performance in team: The multilevel moderating effect of task interdependence," *Journal of Management*, 31, 513–29.

La Porta, R., F. López-de Silanes, A. Shleifer, and R. W. Vishny (1999): "The quality of government," *Journal of Law, Economics and Organization*, 15, 222–79.

Laver, M., and B. W. Hunt (1992): *Policy and Party Competition*. Routledge, New York.

Layard, R. G. (2005): *Happiness. Lessons from a New Science*. Allen Lane, London.

Lerner, M. J. (1982): *The Belief in a Just World: A Fundamental Delusion*. Plenum Press, New York.

Le Grand, J. (2003): *Motivation, Agency, and Public Policy: Of Knights and Knaves, Pawns and Queens*. Oxford University Press, Oxford.

——— (2007): *The Other Invisible Hand: Delivering Public Services Through Choice and Competition*. Princeton University Press, Princeton.

Lipset, S. M. (1967): *The First New Nation*. Doubleday, Garden City.

Lizzeri, A., and N. Persico (2001): "The Provision of Public Goods under Alternative Electoral Incentives," *American Economic Review*, 91, 225–39.

Luttmer, E. F. P. (2001): "Group loyalty and the taste for redistribution," *Journal of Political Economy*, 109, 500–28.

Manski, C. F., and J. D. Straub (1999): "Worker perceptions of job insecurity in the mid-1990s: Evidence from the survey of economic expectations," *Journal of Human Resources*, 35, 447–79.

Meltzer, A., and S. Richards (1981): "A rational theory of the size of government," *Journal of Political Economy*, 89, 914–27.

Milanovic, B. (2000): "The median-voter hypothesis, income inequality, and income redistribution: An empirical test with the required data," *European Journal of Political Economy*, 16, 367–410.

Milesi-Ferretti, G. M., R. Perotti, and M. Rostagno (2002): "Electoral systems and public spending," *Quarterly Journal of Economics*, 117, 609–57.

Mill, J. S. (1859): *On Liberty*. John W. Parker and Son, London, Oxford University Press, 1991.

Miller, T., K. R. Holmes and E. Fuelner (2011): *2011 Index of Economic Freedom*. Heritage Foundation, Washington, DC.

Moene, K. O., and M. Wallerstein (2001): "Inequality, social insurance, and redistribution," *American Political Science Review*, 95, 859–74.

――― (2003): "Earnings inequality and welfare spending: A disaggregated analysis," *World Politics*, 55, 485–516.

Mudambi, R., S. M. Mudambi, and P. Navarra (2007): "Global innovation in MNCs: The effects of subsidiary self-determination and teamwork," *Journal of Product Innovation Management*, 24, 442–55.

Mueller, D. C., and T. Stratmann (2003): "The economic effects of democratic participation," *Journal of Public Economics*, 87, 2129–55.

Murphy, K. M., A. Shleifer, and R. W. Vishny (1991): "The allocation of talent: Implications for growth," *Quarterly Journal of Economics*, 106, 503–30.

Nehring, K., and C. Puppe (2002): "A theory of diversity," *Econometrica*, 70, 1155–98.

Nozick, R. (1974): *Anarchy, State and Utopia*. Basil Blackwell, Oxford.

OECD (2006): *Social Expenditure Database 1980–2005*. Retrieved from http://www.oecd.org/els/social/expenditure/.

Ohtake, F., and J. Tomioka (2004): "Who Supports Redistribution?," *The Japanese Economic Review*, 55, 333–54.

Olson, M. (1965): *The Logic of Collective Action. Public Goods and the Theory of Groups*. Harvard University Press, Cambridge.

Oppenheim, F. E. (2004): "Social freedom: Definition, measurability, valuation," *Social Choice and Welfare*, 22, 175–85.

Pattanaik, P. K., and Y. Xu (1990): "On Ranking Opportunity Sets in Terms of Freedom of Choice," *Réchérches Économiques de Louvain*, 56, 383–90.

――― (1998): "On preference and freedom," *Theory and Decision*, 44, 173–98.

――― (2000a): "On diversity and freedom of choice," *Mathematical Social Sciences*, 40, 123–30.

――― (2000b): "On ranking opportunity sets in economic environments," *Journal of Economic Theory*, 93, 48–71.

Peltzman, S. (1976): "Towards a more general theory of regulation," *Journal of Law and Economics*, 19, 211–40.

Perotti, R. (1993): "Political equilibrium, income distribution and growth," *Review of Economic Studies*, 60, 755–76.

――― (1996): "Growth, income distribution and democracy: What the data say," *Journal of Economic Growth*, 1, 149–88.

Persson, T., and G. Tabellini (1992): "Growth, distribution and politics," *European Economic Review*, 36, 593–602.

――― (1994): "Does centralization increase the size of government?," *European Economic Review*, 38, 765–73.

——— (2000): *Political Economics. Explaining Economic Policy.* The MIT Press, Cambridge.

Pettit, P. (1997): *Republicanism. A Theory of Freedom and Government.* Oxford University Press, Oxford.

——— (2001): *A Theory of Freedom.* Polity Press, Cambridge.

Piketty, T. (1995): "Social mobility and redistributive politics," *Quarterly Journal of Economics*, 60, 551–83.

Poole, K. T., and H. Rosenthal (1991): "Patterns of congressional voting," *American Journal of Political Science*, 35, 228–78.

Popkin, S. L. (1991): *The Reasoning Voter. Communication and Persuasion in Presidential Elections.* University of Chicago Press, Chicago.

Praag, B. M. S. v., and A. Ferrer-i Carbonell (2004): *Happiness Quantified: A Satisfaction Calculus Approach.* Oxford University Press, Oxford.

Prescott, E. C. (2006): "The transformations of macroeconomic policy and research," *Journal of Political Economy*, 114, 203–36.

Przeworski, A., and J. Sprague (1986): *Paper Stones: A History of Electoral Socialism.* University of Chicago Press, Chicago.

Puppe, C. (1995): "Freedom of choice and rational decisions," *Social Choice and Welfare*, 12, 137–53.

——— (1996): "An axiomatic approach to 'preference for freedom of choice'," *Journal of Economic Theory*, 68, 174–99.

Putnam, R. (2007): "E Pluribus Unum: Diversity and Community in the Twenty-First Century: The Johan Skytte Prize Lecture," *Scandinavian Political Studies*, 30 (2), 134–167.

Putterman, L. (1996): "Why have the rabble not redistributed the wealth? On the stability of democracy and unequal property," in *Property Relations, Incentives and Welfare*, ed. by J. Roemer, pp. 359–89. MacMillan, London.

Putterman, L., J. Roemer, and J. Sylvestre (1998): "Does egalitarianism have a future?," *Journal of Economic Literature*, 36, 861–902.

Ravallion, M., and M. Loskin (2000): "Who wants to redistribute? The tunnel effect in 1990 Russia," *Journal of Public Economics*, 76, 87–104.

Rawls, J. (1971): *A Theory of Justice.* Belknap Press, Cambridge.

Roberts, K. W. (1977): "Voting over income tax schedules," *Journal of Public Economics*, 8, 329–40.

Rodriguez, F. (2004): "Inequality, redistribution, and rent-seeking," *Economics and Politics*, 16, 287–320.

Rodrik, D. (1998): "Why do more open economies have bigger governments?," *Journal of Political Economy*, 106, 997–1032.

Roemer, J. (1998): "Why the poor do not expropriate the rich in democracies. An old argument in new garb," *Journal of Public Economics*, 70, 399–426.

Romero Medina, A. (2001): "More on preference and freedom," *Social Choice and Welfare*, 18, 179–91.

Romer, T. (1975): "Individual welfare, majority voting, and the properties of a linear income tax," *Journal of Public Economics*, 4, 163–85.

Rosenstone, S. J., and J. M. Hansen (1993): *Mobilization, Participation, and Democracy in America.* MacMillan, New York.

Rotter, J. B. (1954): *Social Learning and Clinical Psychology.* Prentice Hall, New York.

——— (1990): "Internal versus external locus of control of reinforcement: A case history of a variable," *American Psychologist*, 45, 489–93.

Roubini, N., and J. Sachs (1989): "Political and economic determinants of budget deficits in the industrial democracies," *European Economic Review*, 33, 903–33.

Rubin, Z., and L. A. Peplau (1975): "Who believes in a just world?," *Journal of Social Issues*, 31, 65–89.

Saint Paul, G., and T. Verdier (1996): "Inequality, redistribution and growth: A challenge to the conventional political economy approach," *European Economic Review*, 40, 719–28.

Sansone, C., and J. Harackiewicz (eds.) (2000): *Intrinsic and Extrinsic Motivation: The Search for Optimal Motivation and Performance.* Academic Press, San Diego.

Scheve, K., and D. Stasavage (2006): "Religion and preferences for social insurance," *Quarterly Journal of Political Science*, 1, 255–86.

Sen, A. K. (1977): "Rational fools: A critique of the behavioral foundations of economic theory," *Philosophy and Public Affairs*, 6, 317–44.

——— (1985): "Well-being, agency and freedom," *Journal of Philosophy*, 82, 169–221.

——— (1987): *On Ethics and Economics.* Blackwell, Oxford.

——— (1988): "Freedom of choice: Concept and content," *European Economic Review*, 32, 269–94.

——— (1991): "Welfare, preference and freedom," *Journal of Econometrics*, 50, 15–29.

——— (1992): *Inequality Reexamined.* Harvard University Press, Cambridge.

——— (1993a): "Internal consistency of choice," *Econometrica*, 61, 495–521.

——— (1993b): "Markets and freedoms: Achievements and limitations of the market mechanism in promoting individual freedoms," *Oxford Economic Papers*, 45, 519–41.

——— (1997): "Maximization and the act of choice," *Econometrica*, 65, 745–79.

——— (2004): *Rationality and Freedom.* Harvard University Press, Cambridge.

Sugden, R. (1998): "The metrics of opportunity," *Economics and Philosophy*, 14, 307–37.

———— (2003): "Opportunity as a space for individuality: Its value and the impossibility of measuring it," *Ethics*, 113, 783–809.

———— (2006): "What we desire, what we have reason to desire, whatever we might desire: Mill and Sen on the value of opportunity," *Utilitas*, 18, 33–51.

———— (2010): "Opportunity as mutual advantage," *Economics and Philosophy*, 26, 47–68.

Suhrcke, M. (2001): "Preference for Inequality: East vs. West," Innocenti WP 89, UNICEF Innocenti Research Centre, Florence.

Suppes, P. (1987): "Maximizing freedom of decision: An axiomatic analysis," in *Arrow and the Foundations of the Theory of Economic Policy*, pp. 243–54. MacMillan.

Tocqueville, A. D. (1951): *De la Démocratie en Amérique*. Gallimard, Paris.

van Hees, M. (2000): *Legal Reductionism and Freedom*. Kluwer Academic Publisher, Amsterdam.

———— (2004): "Freedom of choice and diversity of options: Some difficulties," *Social Choice and Welfare*, 22, 253–66.

Verme, P. (2009): "Happiness, freedom and control," *Journal of Economic Behavior and Organization*, 71, 146–71.

Weber, M. (2002): *The Protestant Ethic and The Spirit of Capitalism*. Penguin Books, London.

Weiner, B., and A. Kukla (1970): "An attributional analysis of achievement motivation," *Journal of Personality and Social Psychology*, 15, 1–20.

Weiner, B., H. Heckhausen, and W. U. Meyer (1972): "Causal ascriptions and achievement behaviour: Conceptual analysis of effort and reanalysis of locus of control," *Journal of Personality and Social Psychology*, 21, 239–48.

Wertheimer (1992): *Coercion*. Princeton University Press, Princeton.

Winkelmann, L., and R. Winkelmann (1998): "Why are the unemployed so unhappy? Evidence from panel data," *Economica*, 65, 1–15.

World Bank (2009): *World Development Indicators*. Retrieved from http://data.worldbank.org/data-catalog/world-development-indicators.

World Values Survey (2009): Download Data Files of the Values Studies. World Values Survey. Retrieved from http://www.worldvaluessurvey.org/.

Zaller, J. (1992): *Nature and Origins of Mass Opinion*. Cambridge University Press, Cambridge.

Index

Printed in the United States
by Baker & Taylor Publisher Services